O9-BRZ-800

More Praise for *Tougher Boards for Tougher Times*

"Bill Dimma has made an enormous contribution to both corporate governance and the basic integrity of enterprise in this country with this new book on the role of the Boards of Directors in contemporary business. *Tougher Boards for Tougher Times* should be made mandatory reading for all present Directors and those who harbor aspirations for the office."

~ *James K. Gray, O.C., Co-founder and former Chairman, Canadian Hunter Exploration Ltd.*

"This book illustrates why Bill Dimma is recognized as a leader in the field of corporate governance. Bill has the ability to articulate difficult concepts so that they are easily understood. This book is a must read for all those who are involved, or aspire to become involved, in corporate governance."

~ *Purdy Crawford, Counsel, Osler, Hoskin & Harcourt LLP*

"I can only applaud Bill Dimma's *Tougher Boards for Tougher Times* as very readable and filled with experience and wisdom. It should be read by all involved in corporate governance, from investors to executives and of course regulators and directors."

~ *Stephen A. Jarislowsky, Chairman and Chief Executive Officer, Jarislowsky, Fraser Limited*

"Bill Dimma's new book is full of penetrating insights into the work of the director in the modern enterprise. None is more telling than the recognition that a director's own character is as vital as any definition of independence or formal requirements of corporate governance regulations."

~ *Dr. R. I. (Bob) Tricker, author of the* Economist Essential Director *and first to use the title Corporate Governance*

"All Canadian directors—and shareholders—should celebrate the publication of *Tougher Boards for Tougher Times: Corporate Governance in the Post-Enron Era*, in which Bill Dimma shares his vast experience, his wisdom and his frank advice on how to strive for excellence in what he calls 'the brave new world of directorship in this young century.' It's a great read and an invaluable reference book—I couldn't put it down!"

~ *Mary Mogford, Corporate Director (ICD.D.)*

"Bill Dimma has been actively and positively involved in corporate governance for over a generation. I have always found him well worth listening to—and reading as well!"

~ *The Right Honorable John N. Turner, P.C., C.C., Q.C., Miller Thomson LLP*

"Once again, Bill Dimma has written a thorough and practical guide to navigating the often treacherous currents of board governance. Its readibility makes it a useful handbook for us all."

~ *Arthur Martinez, Former Chairman, President and CEO, Sears, Roebuck and Co.*

"Bill's book is a must-read for both existing and potential Directors. For as the title suggests, joining a Board in today's post-Enron world is a serious, sometimes thankless, but most important challenge and responsibility."

~ *Peter C. Godsoe, Former Chairman and CEO, Scotiabank*

"Bill Dimma's book is a *must* read for every corporate director, particularly for those joining a board for the first time."

~ *The Honourable Henry N. R. Jackman, O.C., O.Ont., LL.D., C.D. Honorary Chairman, The Empire Life Insurance Company*

TOUGHER BOARDS for TOUGHER TIMES

Corporate Governance in the Post-Enron Era

William A. Dimma

John Wiley & Sons Canada, Ltd.

National Library of Canada Cataloguing in Publication Data

Dimma, William A. (William Andrew), 1928-
Tougher boards for tougher times: corporate governance in the post-Enron era / William A. Dimma.

Includes index.
ISBN-13 978-0-470-83730-6
ISBN-10 0-470-83730-6

1. Boards of directors. 2. Corporate governance. I. Title.

HD2745.D543 2006 658.4'22 C2005-906149-9

Production Credits:
Cover and Interior text design: Adrian So
Printer: Friesens

John Wiley & Sons Canada, Ltd.
6045 Freemont Blvd.
Mississauga, Ontario
L5R 4J3

Printed in Canada
1 2 3 4 5 (FP) 10 09 08 07 06

This book is dedicated to all directors, present and future, who take on bravely the considerable and growing responsibilities, challenges, and risks associated with corporate governance in the early years of this century. This is not greatly dissimilar to walking into a den of lions without a chair or whip.

There are few ways in which a man can be more innocently employed than in getting money.

— *Boswell's Life of Samuel Johnson, 1775*

By pursuing his own interest, he frequently promotes that of the society more effectively than when he really intends to promote it. I have never known much good done by those who affected to trade for the public good.

— *Adam Smith, Wealth of Nations, 1776*

The profit motive is not a noble motive. It is not a gallant motive. It is not dignified. And yet it seems useful.

— *Henry Luce, 1952*

Any CEO who cannot outmanoeuvre a system designed to keep him under control is probably not worth having.

— *Anonymous*

Follow those who seek the truth but flee those who have found it.

— *Vaclav Havel*

Contents

Foreword

— *Bernard R. Wilson, FCA, ICD.D*
Corporate Director and Chairman of the Institute of Corporate Directors

LIKE A FINELY tuned athlete, Bill Dimma has once again "hit the governance ball out of the ballpark" with his new book *Tougher Boards for Tougher Times*. Following on the success of *Excellence in the Boardroom*, which is a must-read for any aspiring or experienced director, Bill Dimma has effectively gauged the marketplace and business environment and written a book for today in which he aptly describes the new work of directors as "... demanding, time-consuming, risk-laden, largely thankless and, well, tough and tougher."

The author covers all the post-graduate issues critical to directors, including the new regulatory landscape, time demands, compensation, risk and even ethics; the book is notable for both breadth and depth. However, the publication is made worthwhile by the chapter on "The Director with Character" alone, which should be committed to memory by all, so that everyone can rally around his call to "Bring it on." The book is generously filled with the experience of a lifetime of directorships—a motherlode of wisdom that few can match. This is why so many people respectfully call Bill Dimma the "Dean of Directors in Canada." Bill never holds back and always puts his best counsel and advice on the page for all to benefit from, and I, for one, am truly grateful for another gem to be added to my library—and that of every director, I hope.

I am confident that in this latest book, members of the Institute of Corporate Directors, and also the directors of the future, now have another "must-read" by Bill Dimma, which I know they will come back to time and time again.

Foreword

by Richard F. Haskayne
Board Chair Emeritus, University of Calgary

Corporate governance has always been important to the success of our free enterprise system. One important book, *Excellence in the Boardroom*, on this subject was written by Dr. Dimma in 2002. The new book, *Tougher Boards for Tougher Times*, takes on new relevance as the world has become aware of the catastrophic results of ineffective corporate governance. The most familiar recent example of weak corporate governance is reflected in the Enron case, which has been so widely chronicled. As well, there have been numerous other cases of equal importance in the United States, Canada and Europe. All of these high profile cases have been covered in detail in the press and many of them have been the subjects of authoritative books. *Tougher Boards for Tougher Times* was written subsequent to Enron and does a masterful job of outlining the issues that caused the downfall of Enron and placing those issues in an historical perspective.

Bill Dimma is a very good writer with an exceptional understanding of corporate governance by virtue of his having served on more than fifty corporate boards over a period of more than forty years. I personally have had the good fortune of serving on two of those boards with him. Accordingly, that relationship allows me to comment on this new publication and I am honoured to do so. In fact, I can think of no other director who has the length and breadth of experience in corporate governance issues as Dr. Bill Dimma.

The book is highly readable and designed in such a fashion that, after the first reading, a person can easily identify important subjects which can be used for reference in the practical application of specific governance issues. Dr. Dimma has outlined virtually every situation that a corporate director could face. He explores each issue with a history and an update on current thought. Perhaps of greater import, he provides his own personal observations, based on his vast knowledge and experience in the corporate boardroom.

There are many governance issues still in the process of being resolved, and the information in this book will help readers formulate their own views on these topics. For example, Dr. Dimma does a superb job of discussing the role of the non-executive chairman and covers it in detail, including the time demands on the position and the differences in the philosophical approach between Canada and the United States. I know, having served as a non-executive chairman of several companies, that this subject alone is critical to governance and should be followed closely by directors, particularly those serving on U.S.–based boards.

The controversial issue of senior executive compensation is another difficult challenge for directors, and once again Dr.

Dimma covers the subject in a way that reflects the reasons for some senior executive awards becoming so inflated. His unique approach to the subject is based on many years of handling this delicate matter. He also deals with related subject such as stock options and other compensation mechanisms, including pension benefits. Also included is information on how human resources consultants can be useful, along with a clear explanation of their reporting relationship with the board and management.

Sitting on board committees has become much more demanding in recent years. For a more in-depth treatment of a specialized subject, Dr. Dimma has called upon the expertise of Ken Hugessen to explain the role of the human resource and compensation committee and provide valuable insights based on his own personal experiences.

The role of audit committees has taken on an unusually high profile and responsibility in recent times because of significant overstatements of financial results in cases such as Enron. As a result, the composition of the audit committee has been under scrutiny and significant changes are now being implemented to ensure a much more thorough examination of the corporation's finances. David Smith has contributed an expert chapter covering all aspects of this subject, including views of professionals from the world of finance and accounting.

A third expert contributor, Bob Harding, has contributed a chapter on governance and nominating committees, filled with valuable information and wisdom gleaned from his experience in that area. These three chapters on committees form a little reference section in themselves.

This book offers a wealth of practical advice, based on real world examples, on such important subjects as ethics, social responsibility, interpersonal relationships with directors and management, and the issue of directors' liability. The author even counsels the reader on matters to consider before accepting a board invitation, as well as the problems associated with leaving a board. In my experience, these matters are often overlooked, particularly when people are joining a board for the first time.

Not only will this book be useful for people interested in governance of corporations, it also includes an important section that covers the major differences and similarities between corporations and "not-for-profit" institutions. The analysis in this book will provide an excellent reference for the thousands of people who sit on not-for-profit boards but lack experience with respect to standard corporate procedures.

Because of the practical examples offered on every subject, it would be hard to find a matter facing directors that has not been covered in this book. Accordingly, the book should have wide appeal to existing directors for all types of institutions, as well as officers and employees of those organizations. In addition, it will appeal to the many other stakeholders of institutions that have an interest in governance—including shareholders, bondholders, customers, investors and, in the "not for profit" world, contributors to the organization, as well as those receiving the benefits. All these stakeholders will find Dr. Dimma's insights invaluable.

Another audience that could benefit from this book is that of business students, who at some point in their career are likely to be involved in the governance of various types of institutions. Here, the experience of the author on every governance subject will provide an excellent reference that will stand the test of time.

Having served on twenty public corporate boards over the past three decades, as well as on dozens of charitable and community boards, I can say that this book is a worthwhile read for even the most experienced director.

Richard F. Haskayne, O.C., FCA
Board Chair Emeritus, University of Calgary

Mr. Haskayne's past positions include:
Chairman, TransCanada Corporation
Chairman, NOVA Corporation
Chairman, TransAlta Corporation
Chairman, Fording Inc.
Chairman, MacMillan Bloedel
Chairman and CEO, InterHome Energy
President and CEO, Interprovincial Pipeline
President and CEO, Home Oil Limited
President, Hudson's Bay Oil and Gas Co.
Director of twenty public companies and numerous charitable boards

Acknowledgments

For the ongoing and enthusiastic support of Karen Milner, Elizabeth McCurdy, and Susan James at John Wiley & Sons Canada and of Enid Williams at Brascan Corporation (recently renamed Brookfield Asset Management Inc.), I am most grateful. As I am to Angel Yang who typed several drafts of this book on evenings and weekends with both accuracy and good grace. And I thank Bernie Wilson and Bev Topping as chairman and president/CEO, respectively, of the Institute of Corporate Directors, on the board of which I sat for perhaps ten years, for their continuing encouragement in my authoring this, my second book on corporate governance. And I'm grateful to Bob Harding, Dick Haskayne, Ken Hugesson, David Smith, and Bernie Wilson (again), for contributing a foreword or chapter to this book and thereby adding much value. Also, thanks to several thoughtful and accomplished directors, who shall remain anonymous for fear of omitting some, who have provided valuable ideas and stimulus through discussions of one kind or another. And to the women in my life, Louise, Katherine, and Suzanne, I extend my sympathy to them for putting up with a sometimes distracted husband and father.

Introduction

There are excellent books out there in the market on the formal duties and legal liabilities of corporate directors. This is not such a book, although I touch on these themes from time to time.

In general, I want to focus less on what must and must not be done, much more on processes and behaviour that seek to promote the best interests of the corporation and its shareholders. It need hardly be added that such processes and behaviour must always be fully consistent with both the law and the legitimate interest of other stakeholders.

This book is named *Tougher Boards for Tougher Times* to underscore the obvious. As any director can wryly attest, sitting on a corporate board these days is not the sinecure (or piece of cake for those who prefer metaphor) that it was a generation ago. It's demanding, time-consuming, risk-laden, largely thankless, and, well, tough and tougher. And while director compensation is considerably better than ever before, there are some who feel that it is still insufficient to justify the combination of workload and risk that is part of a director's stock-in-trade these days.

Several years ago, Adam Zimmerman wrote a book with an apt and prescient title: *Who's In Charge Here, Anyway?* In a corporation, where does the buck finally stop? In law, boards hold all the top cards, all the power ... in theory. In practice, they continue to act far too often as if they didn't.

The reasons for this gap between theory and practice will be discussed in more depth throughout this book. But they can be encapsulated in this equation: Knowledge plus time plus resources equal power.

If I'm a CEO, my senior colleagues and I each work between sixty and ninety hours per week. Less doesn't cut it in today's extraordinarily complex and demanding environment. If I'm a director, I attend—let's be generous—eight board meetings and another eight board committee meetings per year at—again, let's be generous—four hours per meeting. This adds up to sixty-four hours per year, plus an equal amount of preparation time for a total of one hundred and twenty-eight hours per year devoted by a typical director to a typical board.

Some boards will, on occasion, demand more time: a company confronting a hostile takeover or initiating a major merger may meet a couple of dozen times a year. Some boards blessed with an environment of profitable stability (a utopian consummation devoutly to be wished!) may devote fewer hours than the average. But for most corporations most of the time, the numbers I've cited are typical.

The resulting comparison is startling. If the typical director devotes 128 hours per year to a corporate board, the typical CEO devotes between 3000 and 4500 hours per year to a corporation. And standing behind that CEO is a dedicated management team plus a rich range of capabilities and resources in terms of both staff and dollars.

This wide discrepancy in time, knowledge, and resources explains why, over the century and a half of the post-industrial revolution era, power migrated from ownership to management. Nevertheless what has evolved is no longer acceptable. And while it is important to remember the old lesson of the baby and the bath water, the lessons from the many corporate fiascos of the past several years cry out for adjustments to the balance of power between managements and directors who represent shareholders and ownership.

While imperial CEOs—at the moment, a breed out of favour but hardly extinct—will fight at every turn against any serious transfer of power from managements to boards, at last the tide has begun to turn. And the direction is as clear as any prediction about the future—capricious as always—can be.

Public outrage is high and is very likely to remain high as the long list of corporate disasters lengthens further. Too many influential segments of society are not amused by the incendiary mix of financial manipulation and outright fraud that has characterized too many corporations. Granted, they represent only a small fraction of the corporate population but still their numbers are far too high. And the sins of the few are visited on the many: distrust is widespread, even of the innocent.

However, there remains a dilemma. On the one hand, if knowledge plus time plus resources to command add up to corporate power, all the laws and all the corporate governance may not be enough to shift the locus of that power as far as it needs to be shifted. On the other hand, the great body of corporate law combines with best practice in corporate governance to make it clear that the balance of power must be shifted. Managements must cede power in critical areas to shareholders through directors acting on behalf of those shareholders.

I note in passing that both the kind and magnitude of shift needed will vary greatly between widely held corporations and those where one or more corporations or individuals are sole or controlling shareholders.

Only quite recently has the pressure to change some of the rules of the game intensified. In their ground-breaking book *The Modern Corporation and Private Property*, published in 1932, Adolf Berle and Gardiner Means identified clearly and early this major shift from owner-managers to hired professionals. But it took nearly seventy more years and the many corporate disasters and senior executive peccadilloes of the last two decades to move public opinion from tacit acceptance of that situation to a strident demand for change.[1]

Several constituencies have finally begun to flex their muscles and to demonstrate increasing clout. Why? Because—to repeat—there have been an unsettling number of outrageous examples of companies ruined or their reputations deeply sullied by power imbalances favouring managements.

The mass media's coverage of CEOs and CFOs doing that infamous perp walk is not reassuring to shareholders and their investor representatives: pension funds, mutual funds, and financial advisors of every stripe.

1. "An era can be said to end when its basic illusions are exhausted." (Arthur Miller) Has it been an illusion to believe that powerful CEOs will routinely put the interests of shareholders ahead of their own?

On many issues of both substance and process, there is the beginning of a shift towards a model—earlier in North America than elsewhere—in which boards predominantly comprising independent directors are demonstrating that they have backbone. When necessary, they are saying NO and they are saying it more often.

Over the past five or six years, considerable momentum has been created by a confluence of powerful forces. These include:

- a broad-based and strongly negative reaction—call it the gathering outrage of public opinion—to senior executive improprieties and serious miscalculations motivated largely by out-of-control compensation systems insufficiently tied to corporate performance over a long enough period;

- the increasingly aggressive, inquisitive, even crusading role of the media;

- the critical views of other outspoken commentators: in think tanks, consultancies, and the punditry in general (the chattering classes);

- the rapid, powerful response of lawmakers and regulators to public opinion and a shaken confidence in corporate leadership and even in the questionable version of the free enterprise system that has become all too common in recent years and continues in vogue to a disturbing extent. At its worst, this version is an unsavoury variant that is well described as rogue capitalism;

- the awakening of that long-sleeping giant, the institutional investor, now at last a force truly to be reckoned with. Both singly and in powerful alliances of like-minded institutions, these managers of immense aggregations of capital have long had the potential but now also have the will to force long-overdue change on corporations and their managements.

Finally—and I hope not least—there is the expanding role of the corporate director and the slow but inevitable movement towards professionalization. This movement is strengthened by the increasing resolve and robustness of national organizations that represent the director class. These include the National Association of Corporate Directors in the United States, the Institute of Directors in Britain, and the Institute of Corporate Directors in Canada.

A highly effective offshoot of such bodies is the education of both existing and potential (soon-to-be and "wannabe") directors. While *training* helps a director understand more about the company on whose board he[2] sits and about its vision, mission, strategy, operations, and people, *education* helps that director to understand better such larger, broader issues as what society expects of its corporations: what is acceptable behaviour and what is not. Of course, education also helps a director to be more effective in helping a corporation reach both its longer-run goals and its shorter-run targets, but especially the former.

2. Allow me to make something clear at the beginning and to repeat what I said early on in my last book, *Excellence in the Boardroom*. Whenever words like "he" or "him" or "his" or "himself" are used throughout this text, they are intended to include "she" or "her" or "herself." The English language, magnificent in so many ways, does not accommodate, except awkwardly, gender-free usage in the singular.

In summary, this book examines the changing role of boards and directors in a tense and uncertain new world of heightened expectations and failed promises beset by wholly unacceptable and egregious excess. In many quarters, there is, to repeat for emphasis, a growing recognition that the future viability of our economic system is threatened by a breach of faith in the way too many corporations are governed and managed at the top.

My previous book was mostly written pre-Enron and in the context of a generally more stable and benign environment. Consequently, it dealt principally with issues of continuity and ongoing structure, process, strategy, culture, values. While this book does not neglect these important continuing issues, it deals with them in the context of a massive change in public expectations and a shift—likely, though by no means certain, to be permanent—in the locus of corporate power. It suits the times that this book is, on the whole, blunter and harder-hitting than its predecessor.

In 1963, I was invited to join my first corporate board. And over the next four decades or so, I've sat on fifty-five boards. A couple of years ago, I was invited by Marcelo Mackinlay, who wrote the foreword to my previous book on corporate governance, *Excellence in the Boardroom*, to share a breakfast meeting platform with Frank McKenna, a fine, thoughtful director who was appointed in early 2005 as Canada's ambassador to the United States. The meeting was billed as a dialogue between two generations of directors. Since Frank had passed the mid-century mark and a little more, I was reminded rather sharply of how long I've been at this director job or trade or gig or—a new and welcome development—*profession*.

For any readers who, like serious baseball fans everywhere, are fond of statistics, I estimate that, since 1963, I've attended some 2000 corporate board meetings and a further 3000 board committee meetings. I hasten to add that these are back-of-the-envelope calculations only. If audited, I shall, depending on jurisdiction, either plead *nolo contendere* or take the Fifth.[3]

If these rather intimidating numbers are recast as some 120 meetings per year or between two and three per week (more in the later years, fewer in the earlier), they seem less formidable, more doable.

Finally, I hope that readers of this book will not be discouraged by the formidable challenges of contemporary directorship. If some of my earlier comments in this introductory chapter convey a message of "Is the game worth the candle?" that is not my intent.

Rather, my intent is to urge vigilance and caution about whether or not to join a given board or, having accepted an invitation, about whether or not it is prudent to continue to serve. My intent is to caution that one should go into a demanding role, where not all risks are charted, with eyes wide open. My intent is to dissuade a director from joining too many boards, should the happy circumstance of a plethora of invitations present itself.

And my intent is to dissuade anyone who will listen from joining a board for any of the wrong reasons, such as the compensation, the false lure of enhanced status or the naïve premise

3. That's the Amendment, not the Glenfiddich.

implied in a comment like "It'll be a great way to make some valuable new contacts and it probably won't take too much of my time."

I hope fervently that the hard work and serious effort that every director needs to put into a board today—in the brave new world of contemporary directorship—will be repaid in the best sense of that word. By this, I mean taking satisfaction from doing an important job, however exacting and risky, and performing it to a higher standard of excellence.

PART ONE THE BIG PICTURE

Chapter 1

The Bad/Good Old Days: Business and Governance Over Four Decades

AS MENTIONED IN THE INTRODUCTION, I joined my first corporate board in 1963, a long time ago by human standards. This raises a couple of interesting questions. How different was corporate governance then? What has changed and by how much? My response—largely personal and anecdotal—follows.

CORPORATE GOVERNANCE

The first time I ran across this term was in the early eighties. If it was used earlier, it was probably only in some arcane scholarly journal. And as for those concepts and precepts embedded in the corporate governance of today, these were largely *terra incognita* even twenty years ago: like the New World to fifteenth-century Europeans.

What passed for governance forty years ago was a group of strong-minded individuals called directors—mostly active or retired corporate leaders—delegating most of their responsibilities to a strong CEO, though he was not yet called a CEO. For the most part, they worked on the assumption that, if any one of them were that CEO, that's the way they would want it to be. The prevailing sentiment favoured a kind of reciprocal back-scratching: you sit on my board but I'll run my company; I'll sit on your board and you'll run your company.

To question, let alone to challenge, even civilly, a sitting CEO at a board meeting was rare—almost, but not quite, unthinkable. To deal with him privately—one on one—was more common. But it was almost invariably recognized that it was the CEO's company and that the key decisions, indeed all decisions, were his to make.

Directors were expected to be supportive, always in public and nearly always in private. With few exceptions, this was how it was. And the exceptions often did not survive for long. "We've talked it over, John, and we think it would be best you didn't let your name stand for re-election."

PROCESS

To say that, in the sixties, directors as a class constituted an old boys' club perpetuates a cliché but, on the whole, an accurate one. At the same time, the senior executive—chairman or president or both—was, as I have already said, almost always completely in charge in public companies without a controlling shareholder. Then as now, controlling shareholders made the important calls.

That class of company aside, the senior executive chose his directors, set board agendas, controlled discussion at board meetings, and generally ran the company pretty much as he chose. Michael Eisner and Conrad Black demonstrate that this isn't so easy these days.

Board meetings were typically short. They often started at 10 a.m. and finished at noon. Going beyond 12:30 p.m. disturbed the luncheon timetable and the executive kitchen. Open discussion was limited and perfunctory. Sometimes the luncheon was longer than the meeting. And while the board format was usually formal and constrained, the ambience, by contrast, tended to be calm, pleasant, even convivial.

THE PACE OF WORK

Although the sixties were a transitional decade, the pace of work for directors was usually sedate, even stately. To some degree, this reflected the pace of society, still basking in the tranquillity of the fifties, the Eisenhower and Saint Laurent years. Competition from Europe and Asia was only beginning to emerge from the devastation of the Second World War. And, in any event, protective tariffs were still high. Communism was a political threat but not a serious economic one.

Boards usually met four times a year, sometimes less often, rarely more frequently. Merger and acquisition (M and A) activity was almost non-existent. That came later, the creation of investment bankers hungry for deals—and fees. The notion that a board might meet two dozen times over a few months to consider how best to deal with a takeover, whether hostile or friendly, was unheard of.

There was a sense of permanence, of continuity, of civilized, even courtly, behaviour, of polished walnut and leather chairs. *Sic transit* ...

BOARD COMMITTEES

The board committee structure was spare. Yes, there were audit committees although some smaller public companies used the board as a whole to perform this role. Only a few companies had any other committees. And even when they did, committee meetings were held infrequently and spasmodically.

The exception was executive committees. They were more common than they are today. Membership consisted mostly of those closest to the CEO. This meant a mix of seniority and cronyism. Often the membership consisted of two or three directors and two or three members of management.

One result, of course, was to divide directors into two classes: those on the inside and in the know—and the rest. This helps to explain why, working with principles of modern corporate governance, executive committees today are gradually being eliminated or are being used only for the occasional need to make a decision faster than the board as a whole can be assembled. Modern telephony makes this largely unnecessary.

DIRECTOR LIABILITIES

Frankly, director liabilities were not much of an issue. Not much attention was paid to them. The chances of litigation against a board were slight. As I think back to some of my earliest boards, I don't recall ever asking about directors and officers insurance. In fact, I'm not sure that most companies even carried it. If they did, it was rarely mentioned and even more rarely needed.

Premiums were painlessly modest in comparison to the king's ransom levels of today, assuming that a policy can be purchased, not always a certainty. Blame rapidly escalating risk levels and litigation costs.

DIRECTOR COMPENSATION

The mantra of the day was "You don't sit on boards for the money." It was considered rather crass even to talk about it. Directors' fee increases were infrequent, but when they occurred, they were treated discreetly, almost furtively. It was less like money earned for services rendered, more like an honorarium paid to a faithful retainer. I exaggerate—a little.

Board membership was widely viewed as a perquisite, a reward, an honour, like being invited to join an exclusive club. Since most directors were active or retired chairmen or presidents—with the occasional exception, perhaps a distinguished university president or dean of a professional faculty, to display the organization's progressiveness and breadth of thinking—it is not surprising that fee levels were considered irrelevant. An analogy might be Bill Gates and Warren Buffet as partners in rubber bridge for a penny a point.

With rare exceptions, sitting on a corporate board was not viewed as a job, a task, a role with serious responsibilities. If someone had used the term "professional director," he would have been greeted with about the same incomprehension that an Iowan farmer might display if an alien spaceship landed on his back forty.

EXECUTIVE COMPENSATION

Even after adjusting for inflation and for societal increases in living standards, executive compensation in the sixties was very modest by today's standards. As has been widely publicized, the multiple of the all-in compensation of the highest-paid to the lowest-paid employee in an S&P 500 corporation has risen from about 40 to about 450 over the past forty years. Similar comparisons in other countries are not as dramatic, but show a similar trend. And, of course, the larger the corporation, the greater the disparity, since those at the bottom earn about the same, while those at the top are able to draw from a larger pot.

The reasons for this persistent trend in widening gaps between working top and bottom are many and complex. Perhaps it is worth noting that there were far fewer executive compensation firms in those halcyon days. It would be churlish of me to note any connection between the work of such firms and the children of Garrison Keillor's Lake Woebegon, all of whom were "above average."

SENIOR EXECUTIVES AND SOCIETY AT LARGE

It seems to me that corporate leaders were held in higher regard in the sixties than they are today. Polls tell us that corporate executives now rank down there with class action lawyers, politicians, and people who phone you at dinner-time to solicit a donation to whatever. Fortunately, drug lords and paedophilic members of the cloth rank still lower. Again I exaggerate—slightly. And while it's true that there are few heroes anymore—*schadenfreude* and the media have seen to that—the businessmen of a couple of generations ago were, on the whole, more highly regarded than they are today.

This decline in societal regard has been intensified greatly by the recent epidemic of scandals and malfeasance. If these are more than cyclical—for every boom begets a new rash of greedy scoundrels—stock options are at least partly to blame, although it's the practice more than the principle that's at fault.

In the sixties, options existed, but just barely. And the upsides were extraordinarily modest compared to the gargantuan grants of the nineties, when obscene amounts were paid out for results—sometimes ephemeral—explained more easily by general increases in price-earnings ratios than by exceptional corporate performance in relation to any reasonable peer group.

It's clear that excessive compensation, mainly in the form of options, has been an important cause of that infamous litany of calamities: reckless acquisitions, book fiddling, fraud, and the final failure, bankruptcy. But it should also be noted that ethical standards are higher than they once were. And tougher regulation makes detection more likely.

A couple of other societal changes are worth a comment. Forty or fifty years ago, most ambitious young men who entered business stayed with one company from graduation to retirement. The attributes most valued were loyalty and stability. Many aspiring executives were content with this; they found it reassuring. Despite the fact that a popular book of those years—William Whyte's *The Organization Man*—portrayed the large corporation's working environment as sterile and stultifying, many were fulfilled and were proud to describe themselves at retirement as "forty-year men."

Or even "fifty-year men," because it was still possible, indeed still fairly common, a couple of generations ago, to "make it" without an undergraduate degree, let alone an MBA and/or accounting and law degrees. I shall never forget a conversation

I had many years ago with a young contemporary, a friend, who decided he wanted to make his career in banking. He was told in an interview with a middle manager at one of Canada's larger banks that the fact he had a university degree did not disqualify him, though it was something of a disadvantage.

ETHICAL STANDARDS

Am I caught in the miasma of nostalgia for what seems to me in retrospect to be a more guileless era when I say that the fifties, sixties, and even seventies were less prone to the outrageous betrayals of investor trust that marred and scarred the last two major upcycles in the eighties and nineties? In those earlier decades, there were, as always, business failures but they were more likely to be honest ones in which companies failed to meet the demands of inexorable change. Often, they were, to use that telling phrase, the victims of past success.

Am I too sanguine, even naïve, about those earlier decades? Several factors make comparison difficult between then and now. The media have become more thorough, more relentless, more able to pierce that well-known corporate veil. And then there's the size of the stakes that, with the advent of stock options, has increased dramatically the incentive to cross that sometimes amorphous but crucial ethical line. And there has been a steady spread of the "me first" philosophy that, despite a growing public awareness of the need for higher ethical standards, has resulted in these being flouted more often.

Once management served shareholders first. Or at least more frequently than today. Now too many senior executives serve themselves first. Most of the time, the two sets of interest coincide. But not always. And despite the earlier and widespread belief that options bring about a happy congruence of interests, "It ain't," to quote Porgy, "necessarily so."

When I'm in Florida, I read an excellent business column by Robert Trigaux in the *St. Petersburg Times*. Not long ago, he published an alphabetical list—A to Z with no exceptions—of twenty-six corporations that have indulged in one alarming variety of major malfeasance or another. He noted that, for several letters, there were multiple candidates. Although many of his choices were American firms, some were not. H is for Hollinger, P is for Parmalat.

Perhaps the evolution of the free enterprise system to the version that is currently in vogue has produced a kind of rogue species and it's time for a new genetic mutation. What we seem to have spawned, not universally but too often for comfort, are individuals who are amoral at best, immoral at worst. They are egocentric, grasping, cynical, and manipulative. And, as the late great professor Ken Andrews of Harvard once wrote, "The corporation is the lengthened shadow of a man."

Is my judgment too harsh? To continue the Darwinian analogy, perhaps those who share my concern and I are like those species veering towards extinction because they failed to adapt to Darwin's dictum about survival of the fittest. Perhaps.

Chapter 2

The Classic Board Dilemma: Individual Competence, Collective Impotence

If there is one governance lesson to be learned from the many corporate calamities of the past few years (and counting), it can be captured in the title of this chapter: "Individual Competence, Collective Impotence." To take only a couple of examples, Enron had, and Nortel had and still has, boards composed of experienced and, in many cases, distinguished persons with outstanding careers and credentials.

And yet, in the case of Enron, the board seemed powerless to prevent blatant accounting abuses and malpractice, as well as massive manipulation and self-enrichment at the expense of shareholders.

In the case of Nortel, the board seemed powerless to anticipate and avert reckless overexpansion and a subsequent corporate implosion with the share price plummeting to a tiny fraction of its high.[1]

1. Later the price rose somewhat but then declined again because of serious accounting problems.

How do we explain this paradoxical combination of first-class individuals and boards unable to get much beyond stunned silence at what went on under their collective watches?

The answer is, in fact, fairly clear but few want to face up to and act on the prescription that flows inexorably from candid diagnosis. To start with, there are several factors contributing to this incongruous combination of individual competence and collective impotence in corporate governance.

THE KNOWLEDGE BARRIER

Especially when the chairman and CEO roles are combined (with or without a lead director), but even when the roles are separated, there is nearly always a profound gap between the depth and breadth of business knowledge held by management and that held by independent directors, including non-executive chairmen. These latter are almost invariably busy people with many other commitments and too little time to overcome the knowledge gap.

CHOOSING DIRECTORS

There are still too few truly independent nominating committees. And, in any event, regardless of the formal structure, the CEO is rarely excluded from the process. The level of influence varies but is usually considerable and sometimes even stronger. Almost always, there is informal power of veto. A director who owes his appointment even partly to a strong CEO is likely to be more compliant than is fully consistent with director independence.

REPORTING RELATIONSHIP AT THE TOP

Consider these two alternatives:

1. Assume the chairman and CEO roles are combined. Power is undivided; the CEO is clearly and unequivocally in charge. The board reports to the CEO in any real sense of the word, though this is, of course, never made explicit nor discussed in polite company. A lead director doesn't change the equation much except to provide the opportunity for a few process refinements such as independent directors meeting routinely without the chairman/CEO present, or board/director assessment.

2. Assume the chairman and CEO roles are separated and the chairman is not the previous CEO or other insider. That is, the chairman is fully independent.[2] In this situation, nominally and formally, the CEO reports to the chairman. *De facto*, this is rarely the case. Rather, they work together collaboratively as partners in an enterprise. Neither reports to the other in actual practice. The relationship is often described as one of creative tension or constructive interaction or mutual dependency.

Nevertheless, the CEO has the major overriding advantage of working sixty to ninety hours per week at his job, while the

2. In Canada, 70 percent of TSX 300 companies separate the chairman and CEO roles. In the U.S., on the other hand, some 80 percent of S&P 500 companies combine the roles. And in many of the other 20 percent, the chairman is a former insider. As a result of the near crisis in corporate governance in the U.S., a number of changes are either in place or imminent. Even on the controversial issue of appointing an independent board chairman, there are early signs of interest. At least the matter is being discussed. I am reminded of Schopenhauer's observation that every truth passes through three stages before it is recognized. In the first, it is ridiculed. In the second, it is opposed. In the third, it is regarded as self-evident.

independent chairman might be able to devote, at best, ten to fifteen hours per week to his.[3] Often it is less, sometimes much less. And because he is independent, he is an outsider and the reins of power are not fully available to him. In short, his role is limited not only by the axiom that knowledge is power, but also by the fact that he has only limited access to the resources of the enterprise, in contrast to the CEO who has almost unlimited access, subject only to broad guidelines.

While chairman and CEO role separation is, in the eyes of many observers, demonstrably superior to role combination, it is not a panacea. The combination of imbalance in knowledge and limited access to resources creates a power imbalance that permits the kind of confidence-sapping crises that have dominated business news in recent years. To repeat Lord Acton's dictum, none the less useful for overuse, "Power corrupts and absolute power corrupts absolutely."

Before I turn to prescription, it is important to note a couple of qualifiers. First, what follows applies principally to widely held public companies and, to a somewhat lesser degree, to public companies that combine a control block, however defined, with minority shareholders.

Let me say unequivocally that, everywhere and always, ownership blocs must be heard and represented on boards and in governance. They are entitled to be heard in proportion to their ownership, though not beyond, on a one share, one vote

3. "Do you mean to tell me that if I work 100 hours a week for 4.3 weeks a month on average, so that I'm working 430 hours a month, some director is going to come in and in three or four hours outsmart *me*? I mean that's crazy! No matter how smart you are, if I work 100 times harder than you on a given subject, you have no way of catching me. No way."—J. Peter Grace, CEO of W.R. Grace, in 1976.

basis. The corollary, of course, is that it is crucial that minority shareholders be represented properly and heard fully.

The second qualifier is that the prescriptions that follow apply more completely to larger companies with a market cap of, say, a billion dollars or more. Problem-solving is rarely costless. Common sense and good governance recognize that, because of economies of scale, smaller enterprises may simply be unable to afford all of the remedies offered here. That does not, however, exempt them from the need to follow best practice adapted to their size and resources.

Some of what follows is no more than today's best governance practice, but some goes beyond. The objective is simple: to increase the odds of avoiding the kinds of major corporate washouts that have made headlines all too frequently.

The underlying problem is, of course, inadequately controlled executive compensation and consequent aberrant behaviour. This includes overemphasis on "short-termism" and the next quarter, egregious levels of stock grants, fringe benefits fit for nothing less than emperors, rash expansion through wildly overpriced acquisitions, accounting manipulation and outright fraud masked temporarily by outrageous complexity and exotic new corporate structures and instruments, abetted by the unprincipled use of insider information.

PRESCRIPTIONS

With rare and temporary exceptions, the chairman and CEO roles must be separated. Combining both roles in one person leads to an unhealthy and, on occasion, dangerous concentration of power. It also leads to schizophrenia, a serious illness. That is, the two jobs are too different to be handled at the same time by one person. The arguments for separation are so well known that to elaborate them here would be to insult the reader and gild the lily.

The chairman must be totally independent and must also have a prior history of independence. He should devote far more time to his job than has usually been the case. In some instances, it is a full-time position or close to it. He is as totally committed in every way to the success of the enterprise as the CEO.

New directors must be chosen by the board, not the CEO. Shareholders continue to approve the slate but in a less perfunctory, more aggressive way. Voting annually for individual directors rather than for the full slate should become the norm.

Institutional investors should take a lively interest in director selection. They must play a proactive role by voting with their minds and not, by selling their shares, with their feet when upset by some governance practice or proposal. Some are already proactive; far too many are not. The Canadian Coalition for Good Governance[4] is an important new initiative.

The CEO reports clearly and unambiguously to the board through the chairman. This may sound like governance motherhood but, when talking about actual practice and realpolitik rather than theory, it is anything but. Half a dozen years ago, I had qualms about this last recommendation that transfers a certain amount of power unambiguously from the executive suite to the boardroom. In fact, I argued against a broadly similar prescription offered by Dave Leighton and Don Thain in articles and books. But that was then and, sadly, now is different.

4. Founded in 2001, C^2G^2, as it is known familiarly, represents a powerful group of large institutional investors dedicated to improving corporate governance and the treatment of shareholders.

This is the appropriate place to raise an important question. Does a redistribution of power by changing and clarifying the reporting relationship at the top of an organization lead to an inevitable loss of either effectiveness (doing the right things) or efficiency (doing things right), to use Peter Drucker's timeless phrasing? To put it another way, does shifting some power from the CEO and management to the chairman and the board imply a cost greater than the cumulative cost of corporate failures through the combination of greed and unchecked power? This latter cost includes the hard-to-quantify but nevertheless palpable decline in faith in financial markets and even, for some, in the version of the free enterprise system that has evolved.

My response to these questions is to observe that an independent chairman and board are far more legitimate and far less conflicted agents of shareholders than are CEOs and management groups with their own personal agendas and axes to grind. Yes, there is some risk of loss of initiative on management's part but it can be minimized so long as it is clear that strategy is a shared responsibility and that execution of strategy continues to remain squarely and solidly with management, subject to sound overview.

Many CEOs and others will, of course, find any change in the distribution of power unsettling and unacceptable. But what is best for management will not always be best for a corporation, for business as a whole, or for society at large.

There are two alternatives to the tough remedies advocated here. One is to increase materially the scope of regulation of all the institutions and individuals in the world of business. The downside is obvious. More laws and regulations inhibit entrepreneurial initiative, smother economic vitality, slow corporate decision-making, dampen freedom of action, and drop the dead hand of bureaucracy clumsily onto the shoulders of the body corporate. Hyperbolic rhetoric? Perhaps, but not too far off the mark.

I view regulation as the default option: to be adopted only after more voluntary approaches have been tried and found wanting. The guiding philosophy, to paraphrase a former Canadian prime minister, Mackenzie King, on Second World War conscription, should be more regulation when necessary but not necessarily more regulation.

The other alternative is continued fine-tuning by implementing various incrementally useful, even necessary, governance changes. None of these deal centrally with the two pivotal realities: knowledge is power and management has much greater access to and control of resources. But at least it is a free-market approach. It combines a healthy regard for letting the market work with the taking of a few necessary, though insufficient, steps to address the most urgent cries for reform. These cries arise out of the Adelphia to WorldCom litany of venality–induced corporate fiascos, with a longer list still to be compiled, alas.

Two or three years ago, I supported this more cautious, incremental approach. But an epiphany occured when it dawned on me that the conventional governance model—take a small step, evaluate, take another small step, if necessary—fails to deal effectively with an inexorable syllogism:

- Knowledge is power; so is access to and control of resources.
- Power accommodates and facilitates venality.
- Far too often, venality is yielded to when the stakes are high enough and the opportunity arises.

Lowering the stakes might help; that is, boards should exercise more restraint on the dollar value of options granted. The expensing of options will help in this regard. But I take only limited comfort from such measures. The stock market and the economy are, of course, notoriously cyclical. And when we're in the sunny uplands where the bull runs wild and the bear hibernates, all bets are off. When times are good, memories are short. And ways to satisfy the needs of the greedy are limited only by their own ingenuity.

Greed will, of course, always be with us. Properly controlled and kept in check, it is an important incentive to accomplishment. But the key word is "controlled" and I fear that incrementalism doesn't get at the heart of the problem. If greed is thwarted by an accounting-induced decline in the use of options, it will be satisfied in some other way. Greed is insatiable and I see no effective alternative to a substantive redistribution of power, as I have argued here.

As an economic conservative, I hesitate before recommending what some will view as bold measures, but take some comfort from remembering something that Aldous Huxley once said, "New ideas begin as heresy, pass through orthodoxy, and end as superstition." At least the first two stages are relevant to the world of business.

Chapter 3

Post–Enron Governance: Early Reaction and Flood of Proposals

IN THE AFTERMATH OF ENRON *et al.*, there was an almost endless flow of remedies proposed by an almost endless number of pundits and commentators of every stripe.

The remedies put forward ranged from sensible and worthwhile, on the one hand, to wonky and unworkable, even dangerous, on the other. This is because those making suggestions ranged widely from solid, experienced business people and regulators, like Arthur Levitt, to an occasional crypto–socialist ideologue, not to mention a crazy or two.

I've selected twenty remedies broken into seven categories. I have tried to choose those that were proposed the most frequently and vigorously, not necessarily those that make the most sense. In short, the twenty suggestions include a potpourri of the sensible, the impractical, and the slightly loony but interesting.

I have, however, excluded some really far–out ideas that have been carelessly bruited about. For example, it was proposed in the U.S. that one–third of all corporate directors be appointed directly by the U.S. government. And it has also been proposed that we eliminate boards of directors altogether and have management report directly to shareholders but with Big Brother—again, the U.S. government—supervising the entire process. My reaction to these two notions is a nervous shudder.

But back to my twenty–item list. I list them each with a brief editorial comment.

CATEGORY 1: BOARD OF DIRECTORS

1. A maximum term should be established for all directors. This should be ten years or age seventy, whichever comes first. (On the whole, I disagree. Continuity, experience, judgment, wisdom matter. A strong chairman terminates non–performers, regardless of age or length of service.)

2. No board can have more than two insiders on it and preferably only one, the company's CEO. (A limit of two management members is fine. But a simple majority of independent directors, in relation to insiders, is sufficient.)

3. The board chair and CEO should be two different persons. Failing that and as a minimum, a lead director must be appointed and given clear responsibilities in certain areas. (In my view, the separation of chair and CEO is much preferable to a lead director. But either is better than full role combination in one person.)

4. Board and individual director assessment should be mandatory. In one extreme version, the director with the poorest rating and lowest ranking each year is not permitted to stand for re–election. Survival of the fittest—very Darwinian. (The principle of board and director assessment, in one form or another, is eminently sensible. Every body and every person must be held accountable. The variant described in the second sentence is too draconian to be useful.)

CATEGORY 2: OPTIONS

5. All options exercised by executives, after permitting enough to be sold to cover the all–in cost of acquiring them, must be held for at least one year and preferably two years before they can be sold. Directors' options, after permitting enough to be sold to cover the exercise cost, should or even must be held until retirement. (I like all of this sort of thing as best practice but not by government fiat.)

6. The use of performance options, in which one or more stretch targets must be met before exercise is permitted, is urged or, in the minds of some pundits, mandated. They have argued that shareholders should not pay for the mediocrity of that now-famous rising tide that lifts all boats in a bull market—in which price-earnings ratios rise for reasons largely independent of corporate performance. (Performance options are becoming more common—thankfully, if belatedly.)

CATEGORY 3: COMPENSATION COMMITTEES

7. In order to exercise more independence and toughness, all members of board compensation committees must be totally unrelated outside directors. (Yes and no. Management attends when appropriate and at the call of the chair. But ownership representing a control group has every right to be present and active.)

8. When board compensation committees require the help of a compensation consultant, that firm must be entirely separate from any hired by management. (This may but need not add costs. It is an essential component of good governance in the area of executive compensation.)

CATEGORY 4: ACCOUNTING ISSUES

9. The cost of options must be expensed each year, reflecting that year's gains. There was, and still is, considerable disagreement about how best to do this. Certainly it is important to avoid double–counting: if treasury shares are used to satisfy option exercise, dilution occurs, reflected in lower earnings per share. (Opponents of option expensing have fought tooth and nail to prevent it. But their battle has been lost—as it should be.)

10. Auditing firms must be rotated on a regular basis. (With only four large international auditing firms left, this is awkward. It's also inefficient and costly.)

11. Or at least auditing partners must be rotated on a regular basis. (This makes much more sense and is being implemented via regulation. The frequency of rotation is more debatable. Some feel that five years, as required in both the U.S. and Canada, is too short and that seven years would be more appropriate.)

12. No partner of company A's auditing firm can be employed by company A for some period, say, three years. Sometimes the proposed prohibition is total. Sometimes it is broadened to include all professionals, such as lawyers and actuaries. (This makes much more sense for accountants, less so, on the whole, for other advisory professionals.)

13. External auditors are forbidden to do any consulting for a client except for work that relates very closely to auditing. Milder suggestions have included the recommendation that any consulting should be limited to some percentage of the audit fee, for example, 20 percent. Alternatively, any consulting work must be approved in advance by the audit committee, which consists entirely of independent directors. (Yes. Variations on these themes are now settled legislation in the U.S. and Canada.)

14. Several accounting policies should be tightened and strengthened, like the treatment of off–balance sheet accounting. The Financial Accounting Standards Board has been considering proposals to consolidate all off–balance sheet activities. Also, cash accounting should supplement conventional accrual accounting that is more heavily influenced by judgment, both

good and bad. (As usual, the devil is in the details. Progress has been slow. Coordination between U.S. and international accounting bodies has been less than ideal.)

CATEGORY 5: TAXES

15. Capital gains on shares held less than six months or perhaps a year should be taxed at full income rates. As a way to make this more palatable to mainstream individual and institutional investors, capital gains on shares held beyond whatever minimum period is adopted should not be taxed at all. (I have to say that I find this one sensible and appealing. It might limit the activities of equity arbitrageurs and day traders, not a bad side effect. Still, I'm not holding my breath. Changing tax law brings out the worst in human behaviour.)

CATEGORY 6: THE INVESTMENT WORLD

16. Where an investment firm has benefited from a financing or an M&A transaction for a client company in the past two years, including any under active consideration, no analyst employed by that firm shall make any recommendation on the shares of that client. (Oh yes! The abuses in this area defy description.)

17. A milder variant is to require the disclosure of all transactions over the past two years between an investment firm and a client company. This would accompany any recommendation on the client's shares by any analyst of the investment firm.

(Disclosure is certainly better than nothing. But too many small investors are too trusting for this to be enough.)

18. Much clearer and less ambiguous language must accompany any recommendation and rating by analysts. Not all investors are experienced enough to realize that HOLD means SELL. Or, as *Business Week* once put it rather pungently, that NEUTRAL means, "Dump this loser and run for your life." (This is best not regulated. The best investment firms have responded to this problem with integrity. Perhaps, for once, good coinage will drive out bad.)

CATEGORY 7: MISCELLANEOUS

19. Serious failures of trust by executives, external auditors, legal counsel, investment firms, and directors should be punished more severely. Jail terms, not merely fines, should be used more routinely, both as retribution and deterrent. A milder variant is to bar those convicted from holding any officer or director appointments for up to life. Disgorgement should be much more common. (As I write this in the autumn of 2005, all of the above is happening. Will these and other steps act as a permanent deterrent? The optimist in me says yes but the skeptic in me says "nothing is permanent but death, taxes and too much duplicity.")

And, finally:

20. Governments should increase substantially the funding of regulatory bodies like the U.S. Securities and Exchange

Commission (SEC) and the Ontario Securities Commission (OSC) to encourage a tougher, more activist line. (And this too is happening, if belatedly. To state the obvious, governments rarely proact but rather react to both crises and lesser events.)

I could go on; the list of suggested remedies is endless. Some have been implemented; some are still being debated. The overarching issue is this: which is the better approach, both philosophically and in terms of its economic and social impact on society, for dealing with the issues raised by the many recent corporate failures of performance and integrity?

One way is to accept that this sort of thing happens and to let the market work and to go with whatever outcome that market determines. This is broadly consistent with Schumpeter's description and approval of what he called the "process of creative destruction." A number of observers, principally businessmen and business economists, have spoken out in favour of this approach as the best response, both philosophically and practically. However, it is more likely to be useful in dealing with honest failure than with dishonesty and fraud.

The other approach is to try to anticipate and avoid serious abuses, even if this means more regulation, tougher laws, draconian changes in the accounting profession and to accounting rules, more red tape, higher standards of governance, tougher penalties for breaking the law and failing to follow the rules.

Those in favour of this approach argue that anything less will turn the public against business and even against the capitalist system. They argue that confidence in the system will remain depressed unless and until strong measures to reassure the public in general, investors in particular, are taken both decisively and soon.

As to which is the wiser road to take, I observe that the Latin poet Horace probably said it best, "*In medias res stat virtus*"—the middle road is best. And so, almost always, it is.

Chapter 4

The Director with Character

WHAT FOLLOWS IS AN edited version of the final lecture to the first class of the Directors Education Program of the ICD/Rotman Corporate Governance College. It was delivered on Sunday, June 13, 2004, just before graduation. The principal thrust of my remarks was to argue that director independence is at least as much a function of individual character as it is of any definitions of independence or of formal relationships.

The most appropriate place for me to begin is to offer my congratulations to each of you as members of this pioneering first class of a new breed of directors.

We all know what the world's oldest profession is, but each of you is now well on your way to joining what may be the world's newest profession: that of corporate director. And this includes those of you who have still to join your first corporate board as well as those of you who already sit on several. I know that a number of you are in this latter category. And if this new profession doesn't represent a massive break with the past and with what directors were and knew and stood for a generation ago, I don't know what does.

At this advanced but never, I hope, terminal stage in your education as directors, it is surely unnecessary for me to retill old ground, that is, to rehash the ingredients that go into the making of a good or even great director and board. That, of course, is what each of you has been immersed in through four modules of three long weekends, along with what I know has been a significant amount of reading and preparation.

You know and I know that best practice in governance is a complex synthesis of many things: board composition, structure, process, chemistry, leadership, culture, behaviour, and values. But it's also influenced, at least to some degree, by a host of largely uncontrollable external variables (what economists like to call exogenous factors).

These latter include things like being in the right industry at the right time—or, on occasion, the wrong industry at the wrong time—and whether the Canadian dollar strengthens or weakens by five or six cents in a given year against the U.S. dollar, and whether the government of the day (a phrase, incidentally, that reminds us of the transient nature of power in a democracy) is helping or hindering and whether that government's instincts and policies in the areas of fiscal rectitude and stable economic growth are sound or not.

Of course, worrying too much about the things we can't control is a recipe for some kind of mental disorder or other.

And, more important, it distracts us from focusing on the things that we *can* control, or at least influence.

One variable that I have not yet mentioned is crucial in determining the worth of a director and of a board. It's described best, I think, by the single word "character." During the U.S. Senate hearings of 2003 on the Enron fiasco, Senator Carnahan, after listening patiently to five hours of former CEO Jeffrey Skilling proclaiming his innocence, finally summed it all up in one blunt sentence: "The bankruptcy of this company does not compare with the bankruptcy of character that occurred in the executive suite."

Character can be discussed and illustrated in an academic setting, especially with the case method, but I doubt that it can be taught. It can be learned but, sadly, only the hard way, by experience, by trial and error, by conflict, and even by failure.

In fact, I believe we learn more useful lessons from failures than from successes. The lessons from success tend to go to our head and cloud our objectivity and insulate us from reality, at least for a time. The lessons from failure stick with us throughout our lives.

This point is illuminated by a brief exchange on the old *Andy Griffith Show* between sheriff Andy and his naïve deputy, Barney Fife. Barney asked Andy how he came to have good judgment. "Well," said Andy, "good judgment comes from experience." Barney then asked, "And where does experience come from?" to which Andy replied, "Experience comes from bad judgment."

And so it does, although it seems to me that not everyone graduates from bad judgment. Perhaps, for an unfortunate few, it's in their genes, which is perhaps just another way of saying that some people never learn.

I'd like to offer a few more comments about character, but this requires me first to go briefly back in time a generation or two. If you'll pardon the impudence of my quoting myself—from the April 2004 issue of *Director*,[1] in which I ruminated on changes in corporate governance over the past four decades, I said:

What passed for governance forty years ago was a group of strong-minded individuals called directors—mostly active or retired corporate leaders—delegating most of their responsibilities to a strong CEO, though he was not yet called a CEO For the most part, they worked on the assumption that if any one of them were that CEO, that's the way they would want it to be. The prevailing sentiment favoured a kind of reciprocal back-scratching.

As we meet here today, we have come a long way from there but we are certainly not yet where those concerned with first-class governance want to be. The best of today's boards may be close but the rest still have much to do.

Too many directors on too many boards have not yet fully shouldered the tougher, stronger, overseeing role that the law and society at large expects, indeed requires, them to play. It's not that directors have abdicated that role; the reality is that they have almost never played it, only rarely and only recently at that.

Which brings me back to character. Directors individually and boards collectively must have the conviction and the strength to say no more often than they do. To start with, the director with character should sniff out the culture carefully

1. And repeated earlier in this book.

before accepting a directorship in a company where management holds all the cards of empowerment. And, even if tentatively satisfied, that director should join with some conditional, if private, reservations. And should resign if it becomes clear sooner or later that the founders and/or majority shareholders and/or control block management are habitually insensitive to the rights of the minority and to the board's obligation to all shareholders.

I might add that the new breed of director should also be wary of entrepreneur–founders who have failed to make the crucial transition to effective managers. Too often, indeed almost chronically, the qualities that are essential in a successful CEO of a mid- to large-cap company are missing in founders. It has taken me several corporate directorships over many years to learn this lesson the hard way. And I confess that I have not always acted quickly enough on what I learned.

But back to character. I believe that it comes down finally to whether independent directors, individually and collectively, have the "cojones" (and, as more women join boards, I should add "or the estrogen") to say to a CEO from time to time: "No."

And when is that? It's when a proposed change in senior executive compensation, even if supported by persuasive evidence compiled by an external consultant with impeccable credentials, is out of line, sometimes outrageously so.

It's when a strategy or a proposed major change in strategic direction is flawed, but a stubborn, strong-willed CEO is oblivious to the weaknesses in what he conceived, even when, as on occasion, those weaknesses are fairly obvious to all but those mesmerized by either or both problems of "forest and trees" and "not invented here."

It's when an acquisition or merger (merger is usually euphemism for acquisition; true mergers are rare) is reckless. That is, it's either overpriced, over-leveraged, culturally incompatible, or name your own derogatory adjective for the three out of four mergers that degenerate into failures.[2]

And it's when an accounting issue, even if unknown to or reluctantly acceded to by the external auditors, crosses the line between fiscal prudence and whatever lies on the other side of that line. That can vary enormously, of course, from moving out of the risk/reward comfort zone but staying near the line, to outright fraud.

I concede that this particular kind of peccadillo is somewhat less likely in the post-Enron era under SARBOX[3] and new OSC rules and regulations. But never underestimate the persistence and ingenuity of that minority of executives with a larcenous streak in their souls.

I should now like to pose two direct questions. Over the past century, have directors slowly but inexorably lost their way? Have they gradually relinquished their obligation to play the vital, active oversight role that was intended for them when the cornerstone structures of the free enterprise system in the post-industrial revolution era were being developed and enshrined in law?

The answer to both questions is largely, if regrettably, affirmative. Fortunately, however, the situation is still capable of

2. Too many mergers involve moving beyond a management's distinctive competence. Isaiah Berlin's line may be relevant: "The fox knows many things, but the hedgehog knows one big thing." Perhaps more hedgehog thinking would avert more misfit mergers.
3. Shorthand for the Sarbanes-Oxley Act, passed rather hastily by the U.S. Congress in the uncertain and nervous economic climate that followed the collapse of Enron and the related dissolution of the accounting firm Arthur Anderson.

being remedied. It is not too late to reverse a hundred years of complacency, passivity, and pliancy, indeed even a willing complicity in the supremacy of management almost always on almost every issue that matters. Or to rephrase that famous mid–nineteenth century toast of U.S. naval commander Stephen Decatur, "Our management! May they always be in the right; but our management, right or wrong."

It is a clear and present reality that other players have moved into the power vacuum created by the failure of boards and directors to take tougher stands when needed. This is definitely salutary. But it's also sobering to realize that this flexing of muscles by other constituencies is an exasperated response to a long history of failure of director oversight. Directors have too rarely grasped the nettle or, to mix metaphors, belled the cat.

And so institutional investors in this country have coalesced to found a powerful and coherent voice in the Canadian Coalition for Good Governance. And it's making a genuine difference.

Governments and their regulators have also responded to growing threats to the ongoing viability of the free enterprise system. Sarbanes-Oxley ushered in a new era and was followed by a Canadian response, milder than SARBOX to date, though not all shoes have yet dropped.

And then there are the media that have been lifting the corporate nighty (or, to put it more delicately, the corporate veil) with ever more vigour and candour. Today, we are accustomed and hardened to stories and photos that would have shocked the readers and viewers of a generation ago. Today, it's largely ho-hum each time we view a stoic, sombre-looking CEO or CFO doing the now-familiar "perp walk" and wearing the felon's chain of office: cuffs around wrists and arms crossed behind backs.

I hope that I am not being overdramatic when I say that the healthy future of the free enterprise system and of investor faith in that system depends far more than many realize on boards and directors with character. This must become the norm not the exception. And you can take considerable pride in realizing that you are or soon will be in a position to participate in and perhaps to help lead a sea change in how boards perform.

Now for the second and last time—that's a solemn promise and I'm not running for political office, which means I'm more likely to keep it—I'd like to refer briefly to something I've written. This time, it was in the *Ivey Quarterly*, the winter issue of 1998. (And I hope, incidentally, that my reference to that other institution, while speaking in these hallowed halls, will be received in a generous ecumenical spirit, despite the rather harshly competitive environment in which today's global business schools operate.)

In that article, now several years old, I argued that directors had no choice but to form and join a profession. I posed three questions that, if they could be answered affirmatively, would help to define a profession in the context of directorship.

First, is there a body of knowledge and a discipline that directors must understand and master in order to carry out their responsibilities fully and properly? Second, is there an essential bond of trust between directors and stakeholders, including, of course, shareholders? And third, do directors as a class have an impact in a significant way on the welfare of society as a whole?

I went on to say that, thirty or even twenty years earlier, the answers to these three questions would have been: (1) not really; (2) yes, though sometimes more *de jure* than *de facto*; and (3) doubtful.

But today, as we approach the summer solstice of 2004, the response to my first question rests with those sitting in this room here and now. You have each embarked on a journey into new territory and taken a big step forward towards acquiring the body of knowledge that is a linchpin in the now-inevitable evolution of directorship into a profession. And the additional steps that most of you will take towards certification will confirm and accelerate this change.

The answers to my second and third questions about a bond of trust between directors and shareholders and about whether directors impact on the welfare of society depend very much on you and on many others who will follow you in the years and decades ahead.

Speaking personally for a moment, I confess that there was a time when I doubted deeply that this watershed transition would ever come to pass. But you and those who follow you, along with those at Rotman and the ICD and the corporate governance college who have organized and taught this splendid array of courses, through which you have now emerged (unscathed, I hope), have turned old doubts into new optimism. The world of corporate governance is in the process of changing permanently for the better.

As I reviewed yesterday evening what I planned to say to you this afternoon, it occurred to me that I may have been overemphasizing the negative roles of the new director: the overseeing role, the gatekeeper role, the judgmental role. Certainly at times, these roles are crucial. And, as I said earlier, it's true that too many directors over the years have failed their responsibilities in these areas. But I do not want to imply that the only or even the most common role of today's director is to say no.

The creative role, the supportive role, the partnership role are even more important when the stars are properly aligned. In fact, these are the normal roles when the board trusts and has full confidence in senior management and when that management is genuinely supportive of a strong, central role for the board and recognizes that the board answers directly to shareholders, while management answers to those shareholders through the board and its independent, non-executive chair.

So, once again, congratulations for making a significant investment of time and money in the future of good, better, best corporate governance. And for being in the vanguard of a sea change in how companies are governed. Perhaps it's not too much of a stretch to call it a movement, one that, if you and those like you stick to your principles, should be beneficial to both society and the economy, as well as personally fulfilling.

To plagiarize John Kerry, who plagiarized someone else before him, my final encouragement to you is captured in those three immortal words: "Bring it on!"

Chapter 5
The Perfect Board Revisited

IN MY LAST BOOK, *Excellence in the Boardroom*, there's a chapter titled *The Perfect Board*. Such a board never existed, of course, and never will. Furthermore, the goal posts have moved in the several years since that material was written. Changing times, changing standards. Today's definition of "perfect," even as a hypothetical construct, is more demanding, more aggressive, more indefatigable, and more unsparing than was likely the case in 2000.

And so it should be, given so many recent, depressing examples of governance gone sorely awry. Too many boards, like deer transfixed by the headlights of an oncoming car, have failed to prevent blatant examples of management greed and excess and their all-too-common aftermath: a lethal mix of fraud and bankruptcy. Too many boards have failed to warn managements early enough and strongly enough about the shoals and sharp rocks associated with reckless expansion, often through greatly overpriced acquisitions. Too many boards have failed to prick the balloon of corporate hubris that, for a time, floated majestically above the gathering risks inherent in a cyclical world where each inevitable down-cycle is marked by hyper-competitiveness and the dog-eat-dog environment that goes with it. You know you're in that zone when you can buy an expensive capital good for nothing down, no interest, and nothing to pay for a year.

In response to investor shock following both personal stock market losses and the painful realization that an unconscionable number of CEOs and others pocketed enormous option gains in advance (sometimes not much in advance) of their companies' share price collapses, politicians and regulators have moved swiftly, especially in the United States.[1]

Laws and regulations influence both structure and process, which in turn can influence behaviour, but only to a degree. Just as the death penalty does not prevent murder, laws and regulations fail to deal effectively with the aberrant behaviour of some CEOs and other executives.

To control or at least to influence behaviour in any serious way requires a clear and unblinking understanding of what motivates it. Once, when the world was younger, executive behaviour was shaped more often by a sense of accomplishment, of doing something worthwhile with one's life, of making a contribution to society, and even by a sense of duty, a word not much in vogue.

And while the senior business people of a generation or two ago enjoyed a good, even enviable, standard of living, they did not, as professional managers, except rarely, accumulate

1. Canadian politicians and regulators have moved somewhat later and more cautiously, torn between the current reality that most of the recent disasters have taken place south of the border and the sobering, high probability that Canada will again, as before, suffer its share of cheats and frauds.

enough capital to retire ten or twenty years early and still bequeath vast sums to their heirs, permitting several subsequent generations to enjoy the privileges of the leisured class.

Today, to put it bluntly, too many senior executives are motivated largely by greed and conspicuous consumption. Like the mantra from the eighties: "I want it and I want it now." That these goals—insufficient at best, ignoble at worst—are more common than they should be is not surprising. In the U.S. in particular, but certainly not exclusively, the strongest manifestation of self-worth is net worth. And a widespread philosophy of rampant materialism—shop till you drop—requires ever more income to stoke unlimited acquisitiveness and the endless consumption of ever more expensive toys.[2]

The urgency to get rich quick and the compulsion to live like a Byzantine emperor mean that the best interests of an enterprise and those of its shareholders are frequently subordinated to the self-fulfillment of those temporarily in charge of it. In a world where celebrity CEOs have been pampered shamelessly, their wishes have too often been boards' commands.

Agency theory argues that the interests of shareholders and executive management must be made congruent. And it has been an article of faith for a couple of decades that this is best accomplished by a mix of stock ownership and stock options, with the mix tilting steadily towards the latter.

But events of the past couple of years have shown that this can have perverse consequences. These include a dangerous preoccupation with short-term expedients intended

2. A few years ago, a Nieman Marcus Christmas catalogue featured a special-edition Bentley for US$700,000 and, for the truly dedicated over-consumer, a US$60,000,000 family submarine.

to force-feed and artificially share price levels and with the use of insider information to cash in before the inevitable reaction: share prices collapsing as they lurch back towards a long-term sustainable trend line ... or lower.

Since this is not an agony column but about governance, allow me to move from description to prescription. In ancient Rome, after the Second Punic War, Cato the Elder ended every speech to the Senate with *Delenda est Carthago*: "Carthage must be destroyed." On a slightly less stirring topic, I like to preface all prescriptive comments on governance with "The chairman and CEO roles must be separated."

It has taken too many massive corporate meltdowns in the U.S. before mainstream thinking there has finally begun to see the wisdom in this arrangement, which, in terms of logic and common sense, is self-evident. Only an overwhelming desire on the part of the majority of CEOs to cling to as much power as society will tolerate has stood in the way of this salutary separation of roles. Once again, a case of changing times, changing standards. Even the *Wall Street Journal*, normally the last bastion of support for CEOs, recently published a compelling article on the desirability of this bifurcation of roles.

Furthermore, the CEO of a widely held public company should and must report clearly and unequivocally to the shareholders through the board chairman and board as a whole.[3]

3. And who appoints the chairman? In a widely held company, it's the shareholders in theory but the board in practice. I realize that the self-perpetuating aspect of this is less than ideal. Where there is a control block, those in control should feel free to appoint the chairman. While a truly independent chairman might be expected to represent minority shareholder interests better, there is such a thing as a tyranny of the minority. Surely the majority has a more legitimate right of appointment. Regardless of who's in the chair, it goes without saying that minority shareholder rights must be scrupulously respected.

Earlier in this book, I referred to Adam Zimmerman's book on directorship: *Who's in Charge Here Anyway?* To which my answer in today's chastened and sobered world is "It's the chairman and, through him, the board as a whole: everywhere and always, as a matter of course."

Bitter medicine for some CEOs to swallow? Probably. And yet I believe it is the capstone of the edifice of effective governance in today's brave new (post-irrational exuberance) world.

Circling back to the "Perfect Board" from a post-Enron, post-Tycos, post-Worldcom, post–name your own favourite corporate disaster perspective, let me list some of the ingredients.

- The board chairman is fully independent. He is not a previous CEO of the company or other insider.

- He works far more hours at this job than has been the norm. In some cases, he works full-time or very close to it.

- He is compensated fairly and competitively. There's no free lunch in strong corporate governance.

- He is clearly not a part of management. He is an overseer of management and the leader of the board which is the central and pivotal intermediary between management and shareholders.

- He and his board work collaboratively and creatively with management in developing strategy. He and his board delegate the execution of strategy totally to management, subject always to that execution remaining true to the strategy in concept and to the business plan in financial terms. And they know early and always when that proviso is not being met.

- The board has used and, when necessary, uses the power to hire and fire the CEO

- The board alone has the power to appoint new directors and, when necessary, to de-appoint them. (If you can de-hire employees, you can de-appoint directors).

- The board—and this is crucial—has absolute power over CEO compensation: its amount, its components, and what hurdles have to be met to earn the variable portion. It is supported by an executive compensation consultant who has no other assignments of any kind from the company or its management.

- Despite all of the above, the board understands and management understands that the CEO and his team are managing the business. No board can manage but all managements must be overseen by an active, committed board that is ultimately and genuinely in charge. That ultimate control must be real and not merely governance jargon that is larded with more form than function.

CONCLUSION

There is much evidence these days that the recruitment of qualified corporate directors is more difficult than it used to be.[4] The

4. A recent study by Mercers showed that director search firms now find that it takes 10 to 12 "asks" to fill a public-company directorship with a fully qualified candidate. A few years ago it took 3 to 4 "asks."

risk/reward calculus is changing; the prestige may be diminishing and the risks are certainly increasing. The sorts of changes described here are essential if the profession of director (and if it isn't one yet, it soon will be) is to remain viable, that is, to make an important, even crucial, ongoing contribution to the success of an enterprise.

Good governance, progressive governance, forceful governance matter. Laws and regulations can help in some areas but board-led behavioral changes, which are only partly influenced by structure and process, are what really matter. Such changes will go a long way towards eliminating the excrescences that have made so many recent headlines.

PART TWO
DIRECTOR INDEPENDENCE

Chapter 6

Director Independence and Definitional Hazards

THE WORK OF THE Saucier Committee[1] was useful in helping to codify best practice in corporate governance. However, like all work in any field of human endeavour, it was not without a flaw or two.

One of these was the categorization of directors. A careful reading of the report makes it clear that what the committee had in mind, based substantially on the earlier work of the Dey Committee,[2] is best portrayed by the following:

1. The Saucier Committee was formed in 2001 under the chairmanship of well-known director Guylaine Saucier. It was mandated by the Toronto Stock Exchange to review and update the earlier work of the Dey Committee.
2. The Dey Committee was formed in 1995 under the chairmanship of Peter Dey, a lawyer and former chairman of the Ontario Securities Commission (OSC). Also established by the Toronto Stock Exchange, the Dey Committee was asked to evaluate the state of corporate governance in TSE-listed companies. It recommended best practice in fourteen areas with a guiding philosophy of "comply or explain."

	Director Designation		
Class of Director	Inside or Outside	Related or Unrelated	Independent or Dependent
Management Director	Inside	Related	Dependent
Director who (or whose Firm) Supplies Services in a Material Way	Outside	Related	Dependent
Controlling or Large Shareholder Director	Outside	Unrelated	Dependent
Fully Independent Director	Outside	Unrelated	Independent

The terms "inside, outside, related, unrelated, independent, dependent" were used somewhat arbitrarily. To describe, for example, a director of a company who is also a member of management of a controlling parent company as unrelated is misleading.

More important, any categorization of directors is most helpful if it leads to useful prescription, such as what number or percent of directors is optimum for each class. Consider each of the above four classes of director:

MANAGEMENT DIRECTOR

As a generalization, only the CEO should represent management on a company's board. A reasonable exception occurs when a successor to the CEO has been named but with a long interval, say, a year, before he takes office. In this situation, the CEO-elect should join the board at naming or, alternatively, no less than six months before taking office.

However, having said that, it is usually a good idea to have all available members of the senior management team attend some part of most board meetings as both observers and participants. The benefits are obvious. Board members get to observe key executives, other than the CEO, in action. And these executives get to interact more frequently with directors, with obvious benefits in terms of motivation, a closer meshing of board and management strategic objectives, and senior executive succession.

DIRECTOR WHO (OR WHOSE FIRM) SUPPLIES SERVICES IN A MATERIAL WAY

The best number for this category is zero. Such a director cannot be expected to voice independent opinions while beholden to management for some part of his income beyond director's fees. Furthermore, on occasion he will find himself in an untenable conflict of interest.

Perhaps someone can think of a legitimate reason for including a director in this class on a board; I confess that I can't. I've heard but discount the argument that a supplier director helps to ensure that said supplier is unusually responsive to requests and requirements. This is a red herring; in today's hyper-competitive environment, any supplier that fails to treat all of its customers, and especially its more material ones, with as much responsiveness and care as it is capable of mustering won't be around for long.

CONTROLLING OR LARGE SHAREHOLDER DIRECTOR

Regardless of what is permitted by law, best practice dictates that a dominant shareholder ought to be able to appoint directors in proportion to its shareholdings up to a maximum of 50 percent plus one. Often such a shareholder can and should be satisfied with less than such proportionate entitlement.

Certainly there is no need for a shareholder with, say, 75 percent of the issued shares to control 75 percent of the director appointments. Regardless of legal entitlement, this is almost always unnecessary. And it deprives that shareholder of a larger number of independent voices and the benefit of more independent views and advice. Such a shareholder is the poorer for parochialism and even, occasionally, for unwarranted paranoia about control.

FULLY INDEPENDENT DIRECTOR

All other directors should, of course, be completely and unequivocally independent. The ideal board should consist of seven to thirteen members. The precise number will vary with company size as well as with the nature of the business and with idiosyncratic preferences of the board chairman and directors.

For illustrative purposes, consider a board with nine members and with a large corporate shareholder owning 40 percent of the issued voting shares. Ideally, this board should comprise one CEO representing management, three or four (40 percent of nine = 3.6) representatives of the large shareholder, and four or five fully independent directors. These latter represent the interests of all shareholders[3] but definitely including the interests of minority shareholders.

3. At least in theory, all directors represent the interests of all shareholders. In practice, the old saw applies to at least some extent: where you stand depends on where you sit.

INDEPENDENT BOARD LEADER

The second area on which I'd like to comment involves the "independent board leader," a term coined by the Saucier Committee to supersede the earlier "lead director," though still to be selected from the board's cadre of outside and unrelated directors. Using the Saucier Committee's definitions and taxonomy, the independent board leader can be either a truly independent director or a member of the management (or other representative) of a controlling or dominant shareholder.

From the perspective of minority shareholders, the appointment of any independent board leader who is not a truly independent director is potentially dysfunctional. In fact, use of the term "independent" for a director who is a member of the management of a controlling shareholder is more Orwellian than the Saucier Committee intended.

Consider a fairly common situation, using as an example a board with which I'm familiar. In 2002, Brascan Corporation had a 71 percent equity interest in Trilon Financial Corporation.[4] Trilon's president and CEO was George Myhal. Its chairman and representative of the controlling shareholder was Tim Price. Both were (and are) able and respected executives.

Some years earlier, a decision had been made to appoint a fully independent lead director. This was done in order to enhance the independence of the board and to respect fully the rights and responsibilities of minority shareholders. As chair of the board's governance and business conduct review committee, made up entirely of fully independent directors, I served as lead director.

4. The minority interest was bought in 2002 and the company name changed to Brascan Financial Corporation in late 2002. It was subsequently converted into a division of Brascan Corporation at the end of 2004.

At the end of every board meeting, the independent directors met privately for anywhere from ten to thirty minutes to discuss any subject raised by anyone present. All relevant comments and advice were passed on almost at once to both the chair and the president. They responded to the independent directors in various ways but always expeditiously and sensitively. Brascan management, Trilon management, and Trilon independent directors unanimously agreed that this division of board responsibilities worked well and added value.

By broadening the definition of "independent board leader" to include a member of the management (or other representative of) a controlling or dominant shareholder, the best interests of minority shareholders may not be represented adequately. This is not best practice. And, as noted earlier, it distorts the meaning of the words "unrelated" and "independent"; a medieval theologian (and Lewis Carroll) would approve.

Chapter 7

Declaration of Independence? Board Composition

IN THE INEVITABLE aftermath of Enron and its doppelgangers, the concept of director independence has been among the more fashionable corporate governance concepts visited and revisited.

It's important to deal with both of two issues in this regard and not merely the first, which is to define what independence means in the context of sound governance. The second issue, once definition has been agreed upon, is to decide what is the most appropriate proportion of independent and dependent (not a very satisfactory term) directors on corporate boards with various ownership structures.

First, then, a brief reprise on definition. In Canada, we have not always been crystal clear in this area. In the Saucier Report, which built on the work of the Dey Committee[1] and

1. The mandates of the Dey Committee and the later Saucier Committee were described briefly in the previous chapter.

made several useful recommendations in other areas, the independence issue was addressed rather opaquely. And so, as described in the chapter on director independence, Byzantine distinctions were enunciated between related and unrelated, inside and outside, dependent and independent directors.

In the U.S., the combination of SARBOX and the SEC/NYSE/NASDAQ constellation (the penchant for acronyms is universal) has, in fact, produced a clear and unambiguous definition. That is, an independent director is one with no ties of any kind, past or present, to a company except his or her director's fees and board membership. That's hard to fault. But I want to make it very clear that the ownership of a company's shares, no matter how many, should play no part whatsoever in defining independence.

In the U.K., the Higgs Report of late 2002 recommended a set of definitions that are at the opposite end of the spectrum from those recommended by the Saucier Report. If applied in their totality, the gene pool for directors would shrink considerably. To illustrate, it was proposed that no two directors may sit together on two different boards, regardless of whether or not there is any connection of any kind between the two enterprises or the two directors. Also, no director may chair two different public company boards, again regardless of a connection or not.

In any event, the climate throughout the world of business is ripe for change and indeed for overreaction to what I grant were too frequent and sobering object lessons in misconduct, malpractice, and felony. At the same time, I like to think that common sense will prevail before any definitional overload is implemented either as new regulation or—more likely in the

U.K. and Canadian governance regimes—as recommended best practice combined with mandatory public disclosure of whatever practice is followed. This approach has been appropriately dubbed "if not, why not."

This leads to the second issue. What is the ideal proportion of independent directors on a given board? To answer this with any degree of satisfaction, it is necessary to separate corporations into two classes: widely held and those where there is a control block. Consider, first, widely held corporations. Here the U.K. model differs substantially from the model commonly followed in both the U.S. and Canada. In the U.K., it is usual for three to five directors on a board of nine to eleven members to be management representatives.

In North America, the norm is one or two. In Canada, for example, the average has remained at two since 1993. The median has recently dropped to one.[2] This is an appropriate and encouraging trend. The same trend prevails in the U.S.

As a personal view, I prefer the North American to the U.K. model, although supporters of the latter argue that a board can make better decisions earlier if the views of the CEO are buttressed by the full-time presence at board meetings of two or three of his most senior and informed colleagues and confidants. Also, the perquisite of a board seat may translate into higher retention rates and perhaps even lower executive compensation costs.

The arguments on the other side are, however, more compelling. First, there is the reality that the CEO's direct reports

2. From the report "Corporate Board Governance and Director Compensation in Canada," a review of 2004 prepared by Patrick O'Callaghan and Associates in partnership with Korn/Ferry International.

are unlikely to speak up much, especially if it means taking a different or even contradictory position from that of their boss. Secondly, what is not needed at board level is a tedious repetition of positions hammered out earlier through intensive management interaction. Any such executive consensus can be explained and defended at board level by a competent CEO alone without the risk of a bulldozing effect and consequent muting impact on the views of independent directors.

This point applies *a fortiori* to smaller boards, a salutary trend over the past dozen years or so, though I doubt we need to shrink most of them much further. With a board of, say, nine members,[3] every additional management director constrains unduly the range of perspectives and views offered by independent directors and backed by a broader set of experiences.

A reasonable exception to having only the CEO as management's board representative occurs when a change at the top is planned and a successor anointed. The other exception, though here the case is not as strong, occurs when there is a COO in place. Depending on the specific circumstances, it may make sense for the COO to be a board member. An example might be when a CEO is close to retirement and it is agreed that the COO will then assume the top job.

Regardless of how many management representatives should be board members, a strong case can be made that most or all of a CEO's direct reports—and sometimes a few others, depending on the agenda for a given board meeting—should sit in on part of every meeting. The advantages were noted in the previous chapter and are obvious.

3. The same O'Callaghan, Korn/Ferry report notes that 52 percent of the largest 293 Canadian public company boards had six to nine members.

Turn with me now to the board where share ownership includes a control block. This leads in turn to the Gordian knot of defining control. It is, of course, well known that, through multi-tiered corporate structures or dual-class share structures, voting control can be maintained with far less than 50 percent of issued shares.[4] In its heyday, Argus Corporation provided an instructive example of control divorced significantly from ownership.

In the interests of space and clarity, I shall confine my remarks to the common situation where there is one share class, and a control block owns at least 50 percent of the outstanding shares. That control block may be held by a combination of one or more individuals, corporations, or trusts. In this situation, the control block has every right to the number of board seats that are proportional to its percent ownership.

However, a control block may choose to restrict the number of its board representatives to less than its proportional entitlement. There is, of course, no risk of loss of control. A board can always be reconstituted, although that would almost never be necessary. An enlightened control block might find it productive to have a high percentage of independent directors in order to gain from the breadth of their collective experience and from their objectivity, judgment, and even—if directors have been chosen carefully—wisdom, a quality chronically in higher demand than supply.

Does and should the control block choose the board chairman? Descriptively, it almost always does. Prescriptively, the arguments in support are at least as persuasive as those against.

4. Magna International, for example, has an extraordinarily large ratio of voting rights for one class of shares in relation to another, namely, 500 to 1.

Furthermore, this does not necessarily exclude a fully independent appointment. Since the true and lasting power resides with the votes, the benefits of an independent chairman, both real and in terms of minority shareholder and public perception, can still be realized. In fact, this happens often enough to attest to the good sense of many control block owners.

Chapter 8

Related Directors: Perception and Reality

At the annual meeting in 2003 of the successful Canadian conglomerate Onex Corporation, its chairman, president and CEO, Gerry Schwartz, proposed adding his wife, Heather Reisman, to the Onex board. This provoked a rather intemperate attack by corporate activist Robert Verdun, who seems to revel in controversial behaviour at many annual meetings.

I was asked for my opinion by a reputable journalist, and offered a view on the principle involved. In the Report on Business section of the *Globe and Mail* the next day, two quotes of mine appeared:

- "In principle, the appointment of a spouse to the board of a publicly traded company 'sends the wrong signal to the marketplace.'"

- "Mr. Dimma said he can understand that controlling shareholders such as Mr. Schwartz may want the support of a family member on his board, but 'on principle, I don't think it's a good practice' because it could raise questions about the board's independence."

Short quotes can never capture nuances and it's an important enough matter to deserve further discussion. The issue hinges, of course, on the right of the owner of a control block to appoint a director of his choice. In the case of Onex, the situation is complicated somewhat by a dual-class share structure. At the time, Mr. Schwartz owned 17.7 percent of the total equity but controlled 60 percent of the voting shares. He nominated six directors to a board of ten members. Mr. Schwartz was, of course, perfectly within his legal rights to do so. Similarly, he was free to nominate anyone he wished, subject to a few excluded persons like convicted felons serving sentences and federal cabinet ministers.

Whether dual-class share structures should continue, from a societal perspective, to be legal is an issue in its own right. If their primary purpose is to buy more time to find a white knight in response to a hostile takeover bid, and assuming always that there are satisfactory coattail provisions in place to protect minority shareholders, perhaps a case can be made for their use in defined situations. It should be noted, however, that a "plain vanilla" shareholder rights plan comes close to offering the same protection.

On the other hand, if their primary purpose is to perpetuate the status quo indefinitely, both dual-class share structures and shareholder rights plan (sometimes more accurately described as poison pills), are usually a contrevention of minority shareholder rights. In both cases, drafting language does not always make clear which objectives and whose interests—management, board, controlling shareholder(s), minority shareholder(s)—are being served.

In any event, dual-class share structures are fairly common in family-controlled and other businesses where there is a control block. If shareholder-approved, they are legal. And so the owner of a control block is entitled to nominate directors of his choice in proportion to the percentage of voting shares that he controls. As a matter of best practice, he should not go beyond this.

To return to the central point and to put it candidly, the owner of a control block should feel free to nominate directors, up to his proportionate entitlement, who will, in a crunch, support him and vote for him. He wants and need directors whom he can trust.

Incidentally, this does not necessarily mean that his nominees are sycophants. In fact, it is not uncommon for related directors to be highly independent in their opinions, if not in their relationships. Sometimes a brother, uncle, or mother-in-law will tell it as it is more readily than an arm's-length, unrelated director. It does, however, depend on the issue and especially on whether control is threatened. This kind of talk may offend purists who often value form over function. But it's part of the fabric of family-controlled enterprises and the *realpolitik* that goes with them.

Of course, a CEO with a control block will be wise to choose directors who bring more to the boardroom than support on demand. He will do well to select individuals who also possess the essential qualities of a first-class director, including sound judgment, broad experience, strength of character, and collegiality.

To return to the Onex case, Mr. Schwartz exercised his legal prerogative to nominate his spouse as one of six related directors. Furthermore, Heather Reisman's considerable experience as a CEO, director, and community leader makes it clear that she is eminently qualified. So where's the rub? Is there a problem and, if so, what is it?

In today's society in general and the business world in particular, three currently useful generalizations are relevant:

- Perception matters at least as much as and often more than reality. The media collectively influence perceptions a great deal and sometimes profoundly. They also determine a lot of agendas.

- Sensitivities about best practice in corporate governance are running very high these days in the post-Enron (*et al.*) environment.

- Opinion leaders as a group, and especially influential members of the press, are holding business leaders to a higher standard. Confidence in business and even in the free enterprise system has been shaken by too many recent, high-profile examples of business leadership behaviour run amok.

Over the past two or three years, the pendulum has swung wide. Some argue that it has swung too far. Perhaps. But if it has, it is a not surprising reaction to a spate of cases that portrayed corporate behaviour at its ugliest.

Conclusion? There is nothing wrong, legally or ethically, with the appointment of Heather Reisman as a related director of a public company where her husband, Gerry Schwartz, holds a controlling interest, albeit with the help of a dual-class share structure.

But such an appointment probably doesn't satisfy the sum of the three generalizations stated above. I cannot say that this is either sensible or fair. But it does reflect some sort of reality in today's brave or not so brave new world.

Postscript

I should emphasize that my comments are not intended to single out for criticism Onex and its highly respected CEO and equally respected spouse. Its purpose, rather, is to illustrate a common occurrence in governance and to draw a lesson from it.

In Canada, where families control a higher proportion of large public companies than in the U.S., the relatives on boards phenomenon is fairly common. I could easily list a dozen and a half large, successful Canadian public companies where this issue arises.

In this modern era of tougher, more demanding corporate governance, public perception matters. And the perception of independence on public-company boards is viewed in many influential circles, including the business press and academe, as important.

Sometimes the appointment of a relative to a board adds strength to that board. And sometimes it doesn't. Sometimes the appointment of a relative is necessary to lay the groundwork for a smooth intergenerational transfer of power. And sometimes it isn't. Regardless, such appointments almost always create a negative public image. Perception usually trumps reality.

While I may not always agree with such perception—its fairness, or lack thereof, depends on the specifics in any given case—I do know that it cannot be ignored except at the risk of a share price discount.

PART THREE

THE BOARD CHAIRMAN

Chapter 9

Differences Between the U.S. and Canada in the Role of Board Chairman. Why?

From time to time, I wonder why more than two-thirds of the TSX companies (presently some 250 of them) separate the roles of chairman and CEO while four-fifths of the S&P 500 companies combine them. This is a significant difference between U.S. and Canadian corporate cultures.

Some of it is probably explained by structural differences; that is, a greater proportion of TSX companies, relative to S&P 500 companies, have a controlling shareholder. Control groups usually prefer to have one of their own representatives in the chair in order to maintain a watching brief and the ability to assert control when necessary. This helps to ensure that a balanced position is taken on issues where the interests of the CEO and management in general differ from those of the control group. Such issues include management compensation and perks, management succession, appointment of directors, and the like. Overall, however, I doubt that structure explains more than a fairly small part of the cross-border difference in chair/CEO practice.

Allow me to return to basics for a moment. It is clear that almost all Canadian commentators on best governance practice believe strongly that the separation of roles is preferable, indeed superior. The arguments in favour are so well-worn in the Canadian setting that I will not insult the reader by expatiating on them at length. They can be summarized in two sentences. When the roles are separated and there is a division of responsibilities between board chairman and CEO, the governance structure is clearer and sharper, better articulated and better understood. Management reports to shareholders through a chairman leading a board that acts as an impartial intermediary and a buffer between the best interests or self-interests of shareholders and management.

But that's prescriptive. In practice and to repeat, the two jobs are largely combined in the U.S., largely separated in Canada. Given this dichotomy, what can be said about its influence on relative corporate performance in the two economies? Sadly, not much. There are too many other important influences at work, including, of course, a huge disparity in the relative sizes of the two economies and of individual companies in each country.

It's true that we start with an unassailable fact. Over most—though not all and not more recent—time frames, U.S. corporate earnings and share price performance, both in aggregate and in almost every sector, have been superior, relative to Canada. Unfortunately, this is almost irrelevant because, as just noted, there are so many differences, some profound, between the two economies. What is needed is a large-sample analysis comparing corporate performance over, say, ten years of companies where the roles are separated and where they're combined. To avoid the apples-to-oranges problem, only U.S. to U.S. and Canada to Canada comparisons should be made.

Although a properly designed study would be informative and useful, I'm not aware that one has yet been conducted. In the absence of quantitative analysis, we are left to hypothesis and our imagination. This encourages me to venture briefly into uncharted waters. My comments will cast no light on the relationship between role separation and corporate performance. For the time being, that line of inquiry appears to be moot. But at least we can try to understand why this key aspect of board structure and dynamics has evolved so differently in the two countries.

One of the more perceptive recent articles I've read on leadership points out that two personal qualities surface time and time again in effective leaders. The first is probably obvious: a strong, unshakeable sense of purpose and direction. The second is somewhat more surprising, at least at first blush. It's a modest, unpretentious, unostentatious personal demeanour and a collegial work style.

This second characteristic seems to imply a leader with a strong sense of teamwork, a willingness to delegate and to share responsibilities, an inclination to share both the glory and the blame, as appropriate. This is compatible with a board structure in which a non-executive chairman and a CEO work in tandem to bring about that creative tension, that collegial dynamic, sought and applauded by good governance theory.

By contrast, the U.S. seems to foster a more individualistic, swashbuckling, "captain of industry" kind of leadership that is less likely to want to share power at the top and is more likely to prefer and even to demand that the roles of chairman and CEO be combined in a single, powerful individual at the apex of the pyramid.

Am I generalizing? Of course. Certainly there are Canadians—I can think of several instantly—who match my U.S. stereotype more closely than my Canadian one. Similarly, we can all think of many successful CEOs of U.S. companies who do not merely give lip service to the language of collegiality and teamwork but practise daily these homely virtues. Nevertheless—and to generalize still further—I believe that the separation of chairman and CEO roles suits the Canadian ethos and character as comfortably and easily as the combination of roles suits the U.S. ethos and character.

Unfortunately, this conjecture does not help to answer the more pressing question of whether corporate performance is helped or hindered and to what degree by the combination or separation of chairman and CEO roles. I'd like to see some bright, young business school professor tackle the difficult but achievable task of collecting and evaluating sufficient empirical evidence to help answer this important question. Then perhaps those of us who speak and write on corporate governance and best practice might address this issue with more assurance and fewer generalizations supported mostly by some mix of personal experience, logic, and gut feeling.

Chapter 10

Time Demands On Today's Non-Executive Chairman

A HIGHLY RESPECTED corporate director and former CEO recently expressed to me some skepticism about my publicly expressed view that the non-executive chairmen of larger public companies need to devote much more time to their roles than has been customary. I have argued that, in some cases, it should be a full-time job.

After much thought, I composed the following response, which, as I was quick to concede, is hardly definitive but is, I hope, at least persuasive.

This is in response to your thoughtful comments on my recent New York speech and my continuing to argue that larger public companies need non-executive chairs who are full-time or close to it.

Perhaps I should say at the outset that my intention has always been to draw attention to the fact that non-executive chairmen need to devote a lot more time to their increasingly difficult and sensitive jobs than many or even most of them have been able to. So there's a little shock therapy in my contention that it's a full-time job or nearly so.

But beyond that, I've been coming around slowly over the past few years to the view that a board and its non-executive chairman must provide a strong countervailing power in relation to the CEO and management of a widely held corporation. That power must be real and not merely titular or symbolic. It can't be like so many companies where the board as a whole has been unable to anticipate or avert the kinds of corporate disasters that have made so many business headlines in recent years.

You know the symptoms and the eventual outcome as well as I: reckless overexpansion, misguided acquisitions at foolish prices, short-term thinking, totally unearned and unwarranted levels of executive compensation, fiddling the books, outright fraud, and bankruptcy.

There are, I think, three ways to deal with these issues:

- More power to boards
- More power to shareholders, à la the Canadian Coalition for Good Governance
- More power to government via tougher legislation and regulations

Probably it will take all three to make a significant difference. Personally, I prefer the first two to the third, philosophically, but some legislative and/or regulatory change has been and continues to be necessary.

But to the extent that boards themselves can be part of the solution instead of part of the problem, boards must exercise more real power, more power to say no more often, more power to provide tough oversight, when necessary, in relation to the CEO and management.

But power without in-depth knowledge to back it up is not real power. Knowledge is power. Without sufficient knowledge, even the strongest non-executive chairman and board are hostage to and relatively impotent or powerless against a headstrong, determined CEO.

So possessing enough knowledge to exert power effectively, on an issue-to-issue basis, is essential. On some issues, that's not so difficult. But on others, it's extraordinarily time-consuming.

Without trying to be too specific, I'd include in this latter category things like:

- Complex acquisitions, especially those in new product markets or into new and unfamiliar geography.

- Major expansions of facilities in existing businesses, based on an economic forecast and an estimate of future demand.

- Determining the most appropriate level of senior executive compensation. This is complicated by dozens of factors and is growing more complicated (and more sensitive) by the day. With whom do you compare your CEO? Where should he fit in any peer-group comparison? Does a reliable peer group exist? What's the real value of an option? Should options be used at all? Can you trust the self-serving studies produced by a compensation consultant, especially if hired by a CEO?

So, it's my belief that a non-executive chairman, if he is to be a truly effective board leader in an increasingly complex world, must work a lot harder and a lot longer than ever before. He needs to be as versed on the important issues and decisions as the CEO. He needs to know enough that he cannot be "snowed" by a strong-willed CEO who may have his priorities wrong.

I realize that some will respond to this by saying that you have to trust your CEO. Otherwise, fire him and find someone you can trust. Such a black-and-white approach may work in a few obvious cases but I think it's often subtler than this and not so simple.

I recognize that two strong people have to learn to work closely with each other. Often this will turn out to be a great productive partnership. In this happy circumstance, the chairman can trust more and perhaps work a few less hours. In other cases, the relationship won't work and it's clear it won't work. If it's because the CEO can't be trusted, a strong chairman and board know what needs to be done and they act.

But in the majority of cases, the truth lies somewhere between these extremes. Things like ego and ambition and power trips often get in the way, but two strong people still have to deal with each other. This is where a strong non-executive chairman, armed with enough power and knowledge to be effective, provides countervail to a strong CEO who, if appropriately guided and, as necessary, controlled, can be highly effective.

To summarize, I have experienced personally some (and certainly know about many) boards where the chairman and directors are in thrall to the CEO and management. Such boards are, as I wrote elsewhere, like a deer transfixed by oncoming headlights. That's obviously not acceptable, not by a long shot.

Power must be shared, genuinely shared. But, for power to be effective, its wielder needs to hold some high cards. And among the highest cards is a level of industry and company knowledge that is both broad and deep. To acquire and maintain in a fast-moving world this level of knowledge is extraordinarily time-consuming. Thus the need for a full-time (or close to it) non-executive chairman.

Recently, I attended a conference at which there was support (certainly not universal) for creating a new job, reporting to the board chairman, called chief governance officer. We have CAOs, CCOs, CFOs, CIOs, CPOs.[1] So why not CGOs? Personally, I would rather focus on strengthening the role of the non-executive chairman without creating a lot of new infrastructure.

In any event, I recognize that the concept of a full-time (or nearly) board chairman is anything but universally accepted. But the corporate disasters of the past several years may require new, tougher measures to help avoid unacceptable repetitions.

1. Audit, compliance, finance, information, privacy, respectively.

Chapter 11

A Larger Role for Today's Non-Executive Chairman

IN THE LIGHT OF SUCH high-profile corporate flame-outs as the ubiquitous and iniquitous Enron debacle, it seems timely to revisit the role of the board chairman in today's more demanding environments. No link in the chain of effective corporate governance is more crucial or defining.

But first let me briefly put things into context. Boards have five responsibilities in their relationship to management:

- To provide a valuable resource to management; that is, to help management achieve excellent results for shareholders.

- To interact constructively with management on strategic and other important issues of common concern.

- To oversee fairly but firmly the ongoing work of management.

- To provide various checks and balances on management.

- *In extremis*, to replace management.

Note that these five roles are arranged in ascending order from more staff-like through mutual partnership to more line-like. Obviously the role mix varies with the state of play in a given company at a given point in time. In the normal course of events, boards almost always are and certainly should be delighted to let management do what it's paid to do: manage effectively and efficiently.

It is a truism to observe that boards must act first and foremost as representatives of the shareholder. On those issues where management and shareholder interests diverge, boards must represent shareholder interests clearly and unequivocally. Fortunately, those issues where there is divergence are far less frequent than those where there is convergence. Nevertheless, the former exist and include management compensation, entrenchment of management rights, golden parachutes, and takeover bids (whether the company is predator or prey).

For a board to play all of its roles effectively, two things are essential. One is full and current knowledge of the issues—both problems and opportunities—facing the enterprise. The other is a consistently high level of mutual trust between the board and management. Nothing is held back. Both bodies act responsibly, maturely, fairly. The board chairman and the CEO each understand and respect the critical distinction between managing a company well and ensuring in every way that it is managed well. All of which is textbook governance. Unfortunately, as noted earlier in this book, there's an endemic problem. Every practicing director knows that it exists and that it's serious. This problem is that it is almost impossible for directors to obtain and maintain sufficient and full knowledge on a real-time basis. Knowledge at this level is held almost exclusively by management. But this dilemma is usually glossed over on the grounds that, since not much can be done about it, "let's do the best we can and live with it."

Directors are, of course, part-time players in the North American context. Consider a fairly typical board which meets five or six times a year and has three or four board committees. Every couple of months, there is an intense flurry of board activity for two or three days. The board meets for a full morning, sometimes for a little longer. Each board committee meets for a couple of hours a day or two earlier. On the evening between the committee meeting and the board meeting, there's a sociable dinner at which some business is often conducted. There are a couple of board lunches.

After the last lunch, the directors depart with a warm sense of having participated in and contributed to something useful. Management—sometimes with a palpable sense of relief, for preparing for board sessions involves a lot of work—goes back to running the business.

Over the following couple of months, the typical director is involved only peripherally. Usually there's an advance copy of a press release or two and perhaps there's a telephonic board meeting to ratify some previously discussed decision or to hear about some new development. But, for the most part, the director is free to pursue his day job and his other, often more demanding interests.

In terms of continuous involvement, this isn't much and, increasingly, it isn't enough. But to be blunt about it, it isn't going to change much for the average director. Boards will meet more often and for longer at a time; this is already happening. But that affects the knowledge problem only marginally.

Which brings me back to the independent board chairman who can play a pivotal role in helping to bridge this knowledge gap. If boards are to be more effective, both in general and in helping to avert the occasional disaster, one answer, at least for larger, widely held companies, is not merely a fully independent chairman but one who devotes much more time to his critical role than has been or is customary. And compensation should be commensurate.

In short, I believe that the next significant development in the ongoing professionalization of directorship might well be a wider use of board chairmen who are both *outside* and *full-time* or nearly so. This may seem, at first blush, to be oxymoronic. It's not. But it is a rare exception in today's North American setting.

In the U.K., the norm is a full-time *inside* chairman, separate from the managing director. In the U.S., the norm is to combine the chairmen and CEO roles in one powerful insider. What I'm suggesting is, of course, different. What sort of person might play successfully the role of *full-time*, *outside* chairman? An ideal candidate is someone who has earned his spurs earlier in his career as a successful CEO, though not as CEO of the company seeking to fill this new role. A wonderful combination (at least in principle: interpersonal chemistry also matters) is the energy, vitality, and forcefulness of a CEO in his forties and the wisdom and accumulated experience of a chairman in his sixties. There will not be a surplus of candidates with all these attributes and credentials.

Would what I'm proposing avoid *all* of the corporate shipwrecks of the past few years, such as Bre-X, Confederation Life, and Livent in Canada or, more recently, Enron, WorldCom, and Tycos in the U.S., to name but a very few of what's out there? Of course not. Would *any* be averted? Quite possibly. If the profession (and art[1]) of directorship could be improved even a little and if an occasional corporate failure could be better anticipated and, therefore, averted, the collective benefits would easily outweigh the collective added costs. For many companies, it's worth serious consideration.

1. It's a profession because it deals with a substantial body of knowledge, rules of conduct, and a range of ethical and other imperatives and constraints. It's an art because it deals with the caprice of human beings and social interactions as well as with the black boxes of the unknown and the unexpected.

PART FOUR
BOARD COMMITTEES

THE NEXT THREE chapters have been written by three guest authors and are concerned with the mandates, responsibilities, and functions of the three principal board committees. These are, of course, the audit, human resource and compensation, and governance and nominating committees. While other committees are important, depending on the industry and company, the three committees discussed in the following three chapters are easily the most common in most public companies.

Incidentally, the wording of the names of these committees can vary somewhat; also, the configurations can vary. For example, the governance and nominating functions are sometimes performed in two separate committees instead of one. However, such variations don't change the job that needs to be done one way or another.

A brief comment now about each of the three authors.

David Smith, who enjoyed a long and successful career as a senior partner and chair of PricewaterhouseCoopers, moved in 2001 to the Canadian Institute of Chartered Accountants as the president and CEO of that 68,000-member organization. He has written the chapter on audit committees.

Ken Hugessen is the author of the chapter on human resource and compensation committees. Ken is with Mercer Human Resource Consulting. He is also one of North America's most knowledgeable, competent, and experienced practitioners in the broad field of executive and director compensation.

Bob Harding, who is chairman of Brookfield Asset Management Inc. (formerly Brascan Corporation), has written the chapter on corporate governance and nominating committees. He takes corporate governance as seriously as anyone I know. One of his principal roles at Brookfield is to ensure that best practice in governance is not only committed to paper but, much more importantly, is practised in every sense of the word.

I hope and expect that you will find these next three chapters as useful as I did. Many thanks to each of them for their collective contribution to this book.

Chapter 12

The Audit Committee

David W. Smith, FCA
President & CEO,
The Canadian Institute of Chartered Accountants

NO BOARD COMMITTEE has received so much attention from legislators, regulators, and the investment community as the audit committee. It was once perceived as a rather dull committee that met periodically and uneventfully with the company's auditors to look at the financial statements on behalf of the board. Now it is one of the toughest assignments for a board member. Audit committee members must meet a daunting list of requirements designed to protect shareholders and other stakeholders from fraud and bad accounting.

The pressure on boards and management to meet investor expectations can be intense. Management will, understandably, use business practices and accounting policies that will achieve and present the company's results in the most favourable light. Audit committee members must be alert to the possibility of exaggeration and distortion of earnings. The committee may have to tell the board things the directors do not want to hear and support recommendations from the auditors that differ from those of management. It must also be prepared to challenge the auditors. In coming to decisions on divisive issues, the committee members will draw on their own knowledge and experience. They also have the right and power to engage (and pay) independent advisors.

Directors may see the requirements for audit committees as being so onerous and technical that they are tempted to defer to the committee and accept their recommendations without question. This can be dangerous because the directors in that case would not understand the scope and significance of the committee's responsibilities and would in turn not devote appropriate attention to it.

It is not necessary for all directors to understand the details of the audit committee's work—it takes a sizeable book to provide detailed guidance for an audit committee member.[1] The directors must, however, know:

- Who should be on the audit committee
- What the audit committee does
- How the audit committee should operate
- How the board should support the audit committee

The material in this chapter reflects the regulatory requirements for companies listed on major stock exchanges in Canada

1. *Integrity in the Spotlight: Audit Committees in a High Risk World,* by James L. Goodfellow and Maureen J. Sabia, published by the Canadian Institute of Chartered Accountants (2nd Edition, 2005) is such a book.

and the United States. Unless otherwise mentioned, the requirements for audit committees are similar in both countries. Directors of other companies, not-for-profit organizations, and public sector organizations may find this chapter a useful guide to good practice but should adapt it to the specific legislation and regulations applicable to their organizations.

WHO SHOULD BE ON THE AUDIT COMMITTEE?

An effective audit committee needs members with the ability and experience to understand and work with the complex and varied demands of their responsibilities. Legislators and regulators are providing increasingly detailed rules and guidelines designed to protect shareholders and other stakeholders.

Independence and "financial literacy" are essential qualifications for audit committee membership. In selecting candidates for board membership, the nominating committee should be aware of the specific requirements that apply to the jurisdictions under which the company operates. In Canada, the securities commissions set the requirements; companies listed in the United States must meet the requirements of the Securities and Exchange Commission (SEC) (including those in the *Sarbanes-Oxley Act*) and the stock exchanges.

All audit committee members must be able to exercise independent judgment. This essentially means that they and their immediate family members should have no current or recent "material" relationship with the company other than as members of the board of directors. Material relationships include both "direct" relationships as employees, executive officers, auditors, consultants, and advisors, and "indirect" relationships as partners, shareholders, and officers of organizations that have relationships with the company. Although there are a number of exceptions to the rules, boards of directors are expected to follow the rules and to identify and resolve any issues that might compromise an individual's independence.

Audit committee members must also understand the financial issues for which they have oversight responsibility. The term "financial literacy" is defined in Canada as "the ability to read and understand a set of financial statements that present a breadth and level of complexity of accounting issues ... that can reasonably be expected to be raised by the issuer's financial statements."

In the United States at least one member of the audit committee must be a "financial expert." The expertise involved includes competence with the preparation and auditing of financial statements, generally accepted accounting principles, internal controls and the functions of an audit committee. To be considered an expert, the individual must have had formal education and experience as an accountant or auditor—a great deal more hands-on expertise than is required for financial literacy.

Clearly, it can be valuable to have at least one financial expert on the audit committee. However, the experts should be chosen for their ability to contribute to the work of the committee without becoming too involved in the technical details. An effective audit committee will generally benefit from including financially literate members with general business experience and a significant understanding of the company's business.

The effectiveness of an audit committee depends to a great extent on the committee chair. This position calls for an individual who is fully familiar with the responsibilities of the committee and is also highly skilled and experienced in conducting meetings. The chair must have the confidence of the board, management, and auditors and possess the courage and determination to pursue and resolve complex and controversial issues.

Audit committee members must spend considerable time preparing for and attending meetings, and may be subject to a higher level of professional liability than most other directors. Companies often consider compensating the chair and audit committee members for the onerous nature of their responsibilities by paying them higher fees than other directors.

WHAT DOES THE AUDIT COMMITTEE DO?

Audit committees today do a great deal more than review the audited annual financial statements. Regulators have widened the scope of their work, which now includes both the annual and quarterly financial statements, Management's Discussion and Analysis, and press releases on earnings. They have also defined the depth and amount of detail the committee must consider.

For companies listed on stock exchanges in the United States, the SEC requires that audit committees review the certification filings made by the CEO and CFO. These certifications cover the annual and interim financial statements, internal control procedures, and fraud. The committee must also review management's report on internal controls and the attestation on management's assertion by the independent auditor.

In addition to these oversight responsibilities, the audit committee is responsible for recommending the appointment and compensation of the external auditor ("independent auditor" in the United States)—tasks formerly handled by management. The committee must also review and pre-approve any "non-audit" services to be provided by the independent auditor. Generally, the external auditors may not undertake certain consulting or tax planning/advisory services for the company, nor may former members of audit teams accept employment with client companies. There are some exceptions and the audit committee must be aware of these. Before recommending the appointment or reappointment of an auditor, the committee should evaluate the audit firm's qualifications (including registrations with oversight bodies such as the PCAOB[2] [USA] and CPAB[3] [Canada]), independence, and performance. To assist the committee in this, the external auditor must provide a written report that can be reviewed at a committee meeting.

Because complaints and "whistle-blowing" by employees and others can provide valuable warnings of fraud and inappropriate activities, audit committees are responsible for ensuring that the company has policies and procedures that record and resolve such information in ways that respect any need for confidentiality, anonymity, and job protection. Some companies provide the audit committee with periodic reports of ethics inquiries, complaints, breaches, and resolutions.

The audit committee's working methods and access to management, auditors, and other experts can make it a useful group to address topics beyond its regulatory responsibilities. Boards may, for example, ask the committee to:

2. Public Company Accounting Oversight Board (www.pcaob.org)
3. Canadian Public Accountability Board (www.cpab-ccrc.ca)

- Monitor compliance with other statutes and regulations
- Monitor compliance with the company's code of ethics
- Participate in the appointment and evaluation of the chief financial officer and other key financial executives
- Participate in the development and evaluation of the executive compensation package and review the proposed amounts for individual executives
- Review the expenses of the CEO and other executives
- Review insurance programs
- Review major consulting contracts
- Review related-party transactions—unless reviewed by another independent board committee

HOW SHOULD THE AUDIT COMMITTEE OPERATE?

Audit committees are required to have a written charter that establishes their mandate and responsibilities. Much of the work of the audit committee involves reviewing and discussing reports from management, the external auditors and (where appropriate) the internal auditors. Regulators do not generally require that audit committees *approve* things but rather that they "review" and "discuss" them. Since the committee acts for the board, which is responsible for the company's stewardship activities and communications, the reviews should provide assurance that the work of management and the auditors complies with statutory and regulatory requirements.

The financial statements and notes require close attention from the audit committee because investors, analysts, and others rely on them to provide a reliable description of the company's financial condition and quality of earnings. The statements must be based on accurate accounting records and present information fairly. The earnings and value of the company are closely affected by the accounting practices used in such areas as the valuation of assets and liabilities, the timing and methods of revenue recognition, and the use of off–balance sheet structures. Audit committee members must know about the systems that provide the numbers for the financial statement and the internal controls that provide protection against errors, omissions, and fraud. They must understand generally accepted accounting principles and be able to assess how appropriate, accurate, and consistent their application to the company's accounting has been.

In most cases, the committee will meet with management or the auditors and include them in the discussion of the reports, although this may not be mandatory. Canadian regulations allow boards and audit committees to establish their own committee procedures for doing this. Companies listed in the United States must follow defined procedures. Under NYSE and/or *Sarbanes-Oxley Act* requirements, the audit committee must meet with the independent (external) auditors to review and discuss:

- Audit problems or difficulties and management's responses

- The responsibilities, budget, and staffing of the company's internal audit function

- Critical accounting policies and practices

- All alternative accounting treatments of financial information that have been discussed with management, the ramifications of each alternative, and the auditor's preferences

- The management letter, schedule of unadjusted differences, and other material written communications between the external auditor and management

The audit committee is also required, under NYSE rules, to meet with management and the external auditor to discuss the annual audited financial statements and quarterly financial statements, including the Management's Discussion and Analysis (MD&A). The MD&A includes information on the principal risks and uncertainties facing the company, the strategies and practices for managing the risks, and the potential impact of the risks on the company's earnings and liquidity. Management's disclosure committee oversees the policy and processes for the preparation and contents of the company's disclosures. In reviewing the work of the disclosure committee, the audit committee should request information and assurance from the external auditors and, where appropriate, the internal auditors and independent experts.

For the meetings and discussions to be effective, the audit committee members must work well together under an experienced chair. A good chair will ensure that the agendas address all the matters that the committee is required to consider and that the committee members get the material they need—which can be substantial—in time to prepare for meetings.

The chair will also make sure that the committee has good working relationships with the board, management, and auditors (both external and internal). An important consideration (mandatory under NYSE rules) is that the committee be able to talk to auditors and advisors in separate executive sessions, without management present.

Above all, the audit committee must be objective and tough-minded. The members should not take anything for granted—and neither should the board.

HOW SHOULD THE BOARD SUPPORT THE AUDIT COMMITTEE?

The board's support of the audit committee is essential. Directors should:

1. Take the time to read and understand the audit committee charter before approving it.

2. Establish and implement a rigorous process for nominating directors who will form the audit committee membership.

3. Appoint a chair with qualifications and experience to lead a strong, independent audit committee.

4. Regularly schedule time in the board agenda for reviewing and discussing reports and recommendations from the audit committee.

5. Participate actively in the discussion of reports and recommendations from the audit committee by posing tough questions to the committee, management, and (if they are present) to auditors and advisors.

6. Be prepared to support the audit committee when its recommendations are difficult and painful for the board and management to accept.

7. Evaluate the performance of the audit committee in conforming to regulatory requirements and meeting its responsibilities to the board and shareholders.

8. Be prepared to support the audit committee's recommendations for the funding of the external audit fees, internal audit budget, and outside experts.

CONCLUSION

The responsibilities of the audit committee, as summarized in this chapter, can be formidable for many directors. But this is not the only aspect of governance with complex issues that affect their work of oversight, approvals, and decision-making. Management, auditors, advisors, and the audit committee must be prepared to provide clear reports and explanations to the board. It's the job of the other board members to support the audit committee, but also to ask tough questions until they understand and approve the committee's recommendations.

Chapter 13

Compensation Committee Competence and Independence: A Work in Progress

Ken Hugessen

IT'S NOW BEEN MORE than four years since the Enron fiasco triggered a series of dramatic changes to corporate governance, from extensive new legal requirements (such as the *Sarbanes-Oxley Act*) and minimum standards (such as those set by the NYSE) to rapidly evolving "best practice" (such as the Conference Board of Canada's standards). Much of the initial focus was on accounting and audit, but attention is now turning to the governance of executive compensation.

While compensation committees have become more involved and accountable for executive compensation decisions over the last several years, and progress has been made against some of the wild excesses of the late nineties, shareholders, regulators, and the public continue to believe that executive pay remains too high, is inadequately disclosed, and is insensitive to downside performance: pay goes up when times are good, and then stays there.

There is more than a little evidence to support these views. Overall executive pay levels continue to climb. Recent "voluntary" disclosure of Supplemental Executive Retirement Plan (SERP) liabilities show the deficiency of current disclosure requirements. The common practice of granting options (or other long-term incentives) annually with little or no regard for individual or corporate performance keeps pay levels high even when performance declines. Today, such practices can be costly, in terms of money, reputation, and shareholder value.

Perhaps most troubling is the apparent difficulty boards have in reducing executive pay in any meaningful way except in a disaster scenario. Stories of CEOs declining their bonuses due to poor performance may reflect admirably on the character of the CEOs, but leave observers wondering why the compensation committee made the award in the first place.

Pay decisions are matters that require the judgment of the compensation committee and board, and test their willingness to make tough and sometimes unpopular decisions,—often under difficult circumstances. A recent book—*Pay without Performance*, by Bebchuk and Fried—highlights how the social and power aspects of board/CEO relationships can frustrate a compensation committee's ability or inclination to balance the interests of shareholders and management in their decisions. To quote, "Boards have persistently failed to negotiate at arm's length with the executives they are meant to oversee. Pay practices have decoupled compensation from performance and camouflaged both the amount and the performance insensitivity of pay."[1]

Central to more balanced pay decisions is enhancement of the role and performance of the compensation committee and the board, including redressing the imbalance of information and resources between management and the directors. In order for compensation committees and boards to be able to act independently and make balanced decisions in an inherently conflicted environment, more work is required in several areas:

- strengthening the *independence* of both the compensation committee members and the processes they follow;

- building the *competence* of compensation committees and of its members;

- ensuring that the committee completes *adequate amounts of research and analysis independent of management;* and finally,

- *enhancing disclosure* to, and communications with, shareholders.

Some observers will dismiss these ideas as a self-serving, make-work manifesto for compensation committees and their consultants. However, there is little doubt that committees that are already following the principles set out in this article (and there are increasing numbers that do), are requiring more work of their members, the chair of the committee in

1. Lucien Bebchuk and Jesse Fried, *Pay without Performance*, Harvard University Press, 2004.

particular, and more work of their consultants. While it is too early to demonstrate a positive result empirically, the sense of the growing number of committees following these principles is that they are making progress towards aligning pay with performance.

Critics of these ideas would do well to recognize that current tactics have been largely unsuccessful in improving the alignment of pay with performance. At best, progress has been sporadic, and in many cases visibly incomplete. Taking on the occasional "bad actor" in the press or at the annual general meeting has had some restraining effect on the most egregious behaviour, but has achieved relatively little towards strengthening the linkage of pay to performance across public companies generally. Neither has it enhanced disclosure geared to helping shareholders understand how much they are paying management in total. It's difficult to see how further progress can be made without addressing the huge imbalance in information and resources available to management versus what is available to the board, in an area of inherent conflict. In summary, if shareholders want something better, they will have to encourage and support directors to do more independent work on executive compensation.

The balance of this article sets out some practical steps to enhance compensation committee and board performance in this critical and highly visible area of overall corporate governance. It follows up and expands on ideas originally set forth in my 2003 article, "Raising the Bar on Compensation Committee Performance," and reflects personal experience gained through work with the compensation committees of a range of large public companies in Canada, the U.S., and the U.K.

The ideas are organized in the following four areas:

- Independence
- Competence
- Diligence
- Disclosure and shareholder communications

INDEPENDENCE

Much attention has been focused on the structural independence of boards, their committees, and individual committee members. Structural independence is important, but independence of thought and process are paramount.

The key to a compensation committee making good decisions is to ensure sufficient and balanced input from both a shareholder and management perspective, and sufficient time to consider and compare. To achieve this, the committee will need to do independent analysis from a shareholder viewpoint in order to complement management input. Pay and performance data should be obtained and analyzed independently from management, and then compared and, where necessary, reconciled with that provided by management.

Many of the problems with executive compensation arise where the compensation committee is overly (or totally) dependent on management for completing its work and making decisions. Some responsibilities in the committee's mandate should be fulfilled almost exclusively by the committee, for example, determining the CEO's bonus. Some other items, however, need only limited committee involvement, for example, approving changes to broad-based employee benefit plans.

But many of the most important tasks, such as setting executive compensation policy or designing a top executive incentive plan, must be done in partnership. While the CEO and the executive team should typically initiate the development of key policies and plans, the committee must be actively involved throughout the process, so as to be able to take unqualified ownership of the end result. Increasingly, committees are initiating reviews, such as a review of change of control or SERP (senior executive retirement plan) arrangements, but the same partnership approach should apply. Setting the right balance between management and committee involvement is key: typically there should be much more direct committee involvement than in the past, but not enough to limit management's accountability for the outcome.

To achieve this and build committee independence, the following principles should be considered:

- Review Committee Charter—should be done annually by the compensation committee for approval by the board, responding to feedback from the board's assessment (typically done annually) of the committee's performance. Input from management and major shareholders should also be sought and considered.

- Determine the year's *meeting schedule and agendas* with direction from non-executive board chair (or lead director) and input from management. Executive compensation has become more complex and the compensation committee's role is expanding, generally requiring more and longer meetings than in the past. The committee should also be prepared to hold *ad hoc* meetings, either with management or *in camera*, as the committee or board deem necessary.

- The committee chair should meet with management and advisors to review any compensation committee mail-out well before its mailing date. This is an increasingly widely followed practice and an effective way of addressing issues prior to the compensation Committee meeting. Committee meetings are more effective if minor differences can be dealt with by the chair prior to the meeting so that any potential major issues are brought to the surface and strategies to resolve them are developed.

- *In camera* should be a standing agenda item at the beginning and end of every meeting. A now widely followed best practice, this allows time both with and without the CEO in attendance, as necessary.

- Similarily, the committee should have available to it regular *in camera* time at every board meeting. Typically, this will not be needed, but it should be on every board meeting agenda.

- Significant changes in executive compensation policy should be considered separately from specific plan proposals. In both cases, these should be considered over several meetings before final approval is provided. Spreading the deliberations over several meetings is essential to allow the committee the time it needs to consider issues fully.

- Avoid approving a plan and an award under that plan at the same meeting. A new executive compensation plan should be considered carefully and not under the duress of the need to make an immediate award or payout.

- The committee must have the ability to assess independent sources of pay and performance data and analysis, as and when the committee sees fit.

Most important is for the committee to control the agenda for deliberations and decision-making. It must work with management, but do enough independent work to form its own views.

COMPETENCE

As important as the *independence* of the compensation committee is the *competence* of the committee members, and in particular the chair of the committee.

All members of the compensation committee should be interested in the topic and prepared to read and attend seminars regularly to keep their knowledge up to date, including attending company-sponsored development sessions specifically designed for board members. Executive compensation is a complex and rapidly evolving area to which many directors bring relatively limited expertise: continuous learning is essential to the effective operation of the committee.

Each year as part of the mandate review, the chair should lead the committee members in a self-assessment of their ability to fully and independently discharge the responsibilities assigned to them by the board under their committee's charter, without undue dependence on management. Knowledge of the basic building blocks of performance measurement and compensation plans, such as equity plans and SERPs, is essential. A clear understanding of the steps required to develop an executive compensation policy, including the choice of comparator companies, the measurement of pay and performance, and the alignment of pay opportunities with performance goals, is also essential. At least one committee member should have industry expertise in monitoring financial and operating performance of the company. They must be comfortable reading analysts' reports and, where appropriate, be able to debate management's choice of performance measures and/or performance assessment reports. Experience with a high-performing compensation committee of a public company is ideal but not always available.

The chair (or at least one member of the committee) should be confident of his ability to discuss the full range of compensation issues with management, without having to defer to management for lack of information, expertise, or experience.

Should the committee determine that it needs to strengthen its own capabilities, it should be able to hire a consultant to provide the required expertise. The consultant should have access to management and any work being done, as it is being done, by management on executive compensation.

Finally, the chair of the committee should be comfortable attesting to the committee's competence, both to the full board and also to shareholders in their annual report. Of course, the full board should assess and communicate the committee's performance annually.

DILIGENCE: ESSENTIAL DUTIES OF THE COMPENSATION COMMITTEE

Having a committee that is both independent and competent is essential, but its overall effectiveness will be determined by how well members apply themselves, and to what tasks.

Success at overseeing executive compensation is premised on doing a few key tasks well, including:

- Maintaining a credible executive compensation policy and, in particular, a credible choice of comparator companies used to provide pay and performance context
- Reviewing and analyzing both *performance* and *pay* on an ongoing basis, not just pay levels
- Developing and managing an explicit pay-for-performance philosophy, including a thorough pre-testing of incentive plan payout levels for various levels of performance. This should be done before a plan is approved and before each performance cycle commences.
- Review the full costs and liabilities of all plans, including providing one- and three-year total "wealth transfer" analysis
- Review and ensure that maximum incentive plan and change of control payment levels are shown to the committee and are reasonable
- Disclose everything—to the board and to the public

• Talking to and listening to shareholders

Even where the committee determines it has the required competence to do its job well, unless a member of the committee has both the time and the resources to conduct independent research and analysis, the committee may choose to use a consultant to collect performance and pay data and to conduct the required pay, performance, and pay-for-performance analyses. Furthermore, the consultant may be asked to provide input and comments on plan design proposals from management, and to test various incentives and other plans, such as change of control.

The compensation committee should continually assess both the competence and independence of its members and its consultant.

The committee should retain direct control over:

1. *Selection* of the consultant

2. Setting out the consultant's *mandate and fees*

3. Providing *feedback to the consultant on performance and value*

DISCLOSURE AND SHAREHOLDER COMMUNICATIONS

A recurring concern among large shareholders (and the public) is that boards are more subordinated to management priorities and pay plan momentum than to shareholder priorities. Shareholders frequently express the view that boards are not responsive to their concerns. Seeking private input from large institutional shareholders is a simple step and provides the compensation committee with a shareholder perspective. In the U.K., shareholders have a non-binding vote on the compensation committee's report on executive compensation, allowing shareholders an opportunity to express their view on compensation committee decisions. While perhaps not appropriate in the North American governance environment, this does help ensure that the compensation committee is hearing from the owners.

Boards must provide an attestation to the committee's competence and access to the resources required to satisfactorily fulfill the committee's mandate.

Finally, boards must, of course, be prepared to explain the committee's process decisions at annual general meetings.

CONCLUSION

Building independence and competence, and doing the required work, are the cornerstones of better executive compensation governance by both the compensation committee and the board as a whole. Through the careful preservation of an independent process, a commitment to continuous learning, and hard work, the compensation committee can produce more even-handed results for both management and shareholders.

Chapter 14

The Governance and Nominating Committee

Robert J. Harding
Chairman, Brookfield Asset Management Inc.

NUMEROUS BOOKS and articles have been written on the topic of corporate governance over the past few years, providing us with a wealth of knowledge and advice on how corporations should structure the board to enhance its operations and hence improve the overall governance of the corporation. We have all received the latest list of "best practices" to follow and most boards have made major strides in reviewing their practices, which has resulted in better boards and more rigorous oversight of the operations of the board and the corporations they serve.

In this chapter, I do not intend to set out yet another list of what boards or their governance and nominating committees should do to provide better governance, but rather will examine some of the more difficult issues that I believe boards are still struggling to address. In particular, this chapter will focus on those areas that fall within the responsibility of the governance and nominating committee and provide some suggestions on an effective means of addressing these difficult issues.

To start, as the name of the committee suggests, the governance and nominating committee performs two functions. The first is the oversight of the corporate governance policies and procedures of the corporation. With the introduction of the *Sarbanes-Oxley Act* of 2002 in the U.S., the Toronto Stock Exchange (TSX) Governance Guidelines in Canada, and the recently issued Ontario Securities Commission "National Policy 58-201 Corporate Governance Guidelines," most publicly-listed corporations now have well-established corporate governance policies and procedures in place. Therefore, this function of the governance and nominating committee is likely being carried out effectively by the majority of governance and nominating committees in North America today.

The second function that the governance and nominating committee performs is selecting candidates to serve as directors and recommending them to the corporation's shareholders. It is the performance of this function that I believe many boards are still looking to improve. Building a better board takes a considerable amount of time and effort and must be done in an environment of trust and candour. Given the increased demands and risks associated with being a corporate director, the pool of willing talent is shrinking, making the task of finding new directors more difficult today and compounding the difficulty of growing a more effective board of directors.

How governance and nominating committees perform both of these functions will have a significant impact on the governance of the corporation. However, before getting into the discussion of the more challenging issues facing governance and nominating committees, I would first like to share one observation that should prelude any discussion on corporate governance. In my view, one of the most important elements of corporate governance, and one

I do not believe gets enough "air time" in the debate on corporate governance, is the concept of "Tone at the Top." Often we hear of this concept as it relates to senior management of the corporation, but optimally it must start with the board of directors. Whenever a board of directors considers making changes to the governance policies and procedures of a corporation or considers new candidates for election to the board, it should be mindful how these changes will affect the culture and "Tone at the Top" of the corporation, that is, the board of directors.

Considering the amount of time and effort most boards have devoted to improving their corporate governance policies and procedures, I believe there remain only a few areas with which boards continue to struggle. The role and responsibilities of both the audit committee and the human resources and compensation committees are well established. This has resulted in improved financial reporting and enhanced rigour in how boards set compensation and in how compensation is disclosed. The areas most boards are still finding difficult to crystallize relate to functions usually considered to be within the scope of the governance and nominating committee's responsibilities and, more particularly, the nominating and board development functions.

In talking with other board chairs and governance experts, my sense is that there are two issues that keep surfacing for discussion. The first is how to make changes to the composition of the board. The second is how to effectively evaluate the performance of the board and individual directors and follow up with meaningful change. Clearly, both of these issues are generally considered to fall within the responsibility of the governance and nominating committee.

Changing the composition of a board is one of the most difficult tasks a governance and nominating committee will have to execute. The difficulty arises because most boards are already well-established and most directors have served for a number of years. These directors are comfortable with and know one another and they are generally viewed as senior members of the business community. It has also generally not been considered necessary to make changes to a board, even if the nature of a given corporation has itself changed. Making a change to the board frequently corresponds to asking a board member not to stand for re-election. Such a request is often a thorny task unless a well-thought-out process is in place.

In order to begin to address the board composition issue, the first hurdle that boards and individual directors will need to overcome is their negative concept of change to the board. They will need to openly accept and agree that change is sometimes necessary. While this may seem like an obvious evolution given today's governance-focused environment, past practices often make it difficult for a board and individual directors to accept that the need to make changes is not generally a reflection on the skills or dedication of any director. Rather, it is about the right mix of skills, perspectives and synergies.

In the past, the job of asking a director to leave the board has usually been left solely to the board chair, with little if any input from other directors. Traditionally, the chair would simply advise the board that the relevant director would not be standing for re-election, leaving the impression that the departing director was underperforming or had asked too many questions.

In fact, there can be any number of reasons that would cause the board to consider making changes to its composition. In today's business environment, the nature of a corporation's business is constantly changing and adjusting to new challenges, new competition, and new products. Therefore, it stands to reason that the type of board and the talents and skills required of directors will also change if the corporation is going to successfully anticipate and react to these changes. Once a board can accept that it is not a fixed entity, the path is clear for a more open and productive discussion of what changes are necessary and how best to implement them.

Having cleared the first hurdle, the next step for the governance and nominating committee is to engage the board and senior management in a serious discussion of what type of board is appropriate for the corporation. One of the most frequently used expressions in governance today is "the board is very engaged." But what does this mean? To create an effective board, the directors must first discuss and agree on what level of engagement is appropriate in the current circumstances. It will also be important to ensure that the corporation's senior management agrees with the board's assessment of the level of engagement that it will have in the affairs of the corporation. Not surprisingly, the board and management might have different opinions in this regard. Reaching agreement is critical to building an effective board and a constructive working relationship with senior management.

A number of factors will impact the level of involvement the board will have in the corporation's business. Some questions to consider include, but are not limited to:

- How mature is the business of the corporation?
- Is it a start-up?
- Does the corporation have a seasoned and experienced senior management team?
- Is the corporation in financial difficulty?
- Is the corporation operating a heavily-regulated business or multiple lines of business?
- Does the corporation have a significant or controlling shareholder?

For most corporations, an engaged board is one that provides oversight and support to the corporation's management by giving advice on major issues and strategic initiatives, oversees management, and judges the performance of the management team against predetermined criteria.

The answers to the questions listed above will likely influence the level of engagement that directors believe they should have in the actual operations of the corporation. By first assessing the level of involvement that the board feels is necessary and ensuring that management agrees with this assessment, the board will be better equipped to assess what composition the board should have. All boards need to strike the right balance between overseeing the management of the company and actually being involved in the day-to-day operations.

Having agreed that some level of change may be necessary and having determined what type of board, or level of engagement, is appropriate in the circumstances, the foundation is now in place to proceed to build a better board. The next step is to consider what the composition of the board should be. This requires examining the skills, competencies, diversity and any other elements that the board believes would enhance its effectiveness. Over the past few years, we have seen most boards develop a skills matrix identifying the skills and competencies the board needs, and comparing these against the talents of the existing directors. This has become an effective tool for providing a gap analysis and a starting point for making changes to the composition of the board.

While this is clearly a useful exercise, governance and nominating committees will need to be sure that they do not become too rigid in setting out the skills and competencies they believe the board should possess. When we think of skills, we usually consider aptitudes such as independence, specific industry experience, communications skills, legal or accounting expertise, corporate finance experience and so on. Each of these is a very specific skill set. However, governance and nominating committees must also consider some softer skills that are equally important in building an effective board. These are qualities that I suggest can be thought of as behavioural skills: diligence, ethics, questioning, demanding, collegiality, respect and so on. These characteristics are just as important as the specific skill sets, because they will generally influence the culture of the board and thus the "Tone at the Top."

By creating an environment in the boardroom that acknowledges the need to constantly consider the need for change, by regularly reviewing the type of board required in the particular circumstances, and by having a well-developed skills matrix which includes specific skills as well as behavioral characteristics, governance and nominating committees will be better equipped to ensure they have the right mix of individuals as directors. These tools will also make it easier for the governance and nominating committee, as well as each individual director, to consider on a regular basis the appropriateness of any director's membership on the board. In fact, if the right environment exists, most individuals are more likely to assess their own position on the board and be forthcoming when they feel the time is right for them to consider leaving the board, making it easier for boards to rebalance the skill mix. This type of open process transforms the responsibility for initiating change from one solely performed by the governance and nominating committee to one which is shared by each individual director, working together with the governance and nominating committee.

The shift in corporate governance practices over the past few years has undoubtedly improved the way boards function. Being a corporate director is now a serious job and not merely membership in a club. However, there has been one notable downside to these changes. The increased emphasis on independence, the need to have financial experts on the audit committee, the significantly greater time commitment for directors, and the risk associated with being a director, have cumulatively resulted in a significantly diminished pool of individuals willing to serve as corporate directors. Add to this the fact that most corporations now limit the number of boards on which a director can sit, and the fact that most CEOs are allowed to sit on only one outside board, if any, and it becomes very clear that boards now need to think differently and creatively about where they look to find new directors.

One observation on this point is that many boards still consider it necessary to have a mandatory retirement age for directors. In contrast, my experience suggests that one of the best sources for new directors is to look for individuals who have had a wealth of experience in a variety of circumstances. Individuals who have been tested during difficult times can often bring a valuable viewpoint to any board discussion. Who would better fit this description than our young senior citizens! As many have observed, today's 70-year-olds are the new 60-year-olds! With all the advances in governance to date, I believe mandatory retirement based on age is a thing of the past. (Just in case the reader is wondering if my perspective betrays a burgeoning self-interest to keep a board seat, let me assure you that my golden years are still a long way off.)

The second area with which boards continue to struggle is the issue of board evaluations. Obviously this is closely linked to the first topic I discussed, making changes to the board. In fact, if done correctly, board and individual director evaluations can be an effective tool that can help in building a better board. Commencing the introspective process of self-evaluations has not been an easy task for boards for the obvious reason that it is quite different from the culture previously found in the boardrooms of most corporations, a culture that analyzes others and factors external to the board. It will take time to implement the self-evaluation process effectively and to socialize boards and directors to such a process. Boards will have 'to learn to walk before they run'. Most corporations have taken the first step and have started doing overall board evaluations over the past few years. Today, most boards and are doing reasonably well in conducting overall assessments of the board collectively and in assessing of the various committees of the board.

These overall board assessments are generally done through the use of formal board evaluation questionnaires. Such questionnaires usually focus on the board's responsibilities as set out in the written board and board committee mandates and provide a good assessment of how well the board is doing at fulfilling its formal responsibilities. And, given the focus on governance over the past few years, I would suggest that most boards now find they are doing well and, rightly so, are giving themselves good marks.

However, I think boards are now struggling with moving to the next step: how to conduct individual director assessments, how to provide constructive feedback to individual directors and, finally, how to implement an effective system to ensure that any feedback is actioned. Numerous surveys have indicated that a high percentage of directors feel that individual assessments should be done, even though only a small percentage of boards in fact do them. Why then are boards so reluctant to perform individual director evaluations? I think this reluctance is on account of a perception that the purpose of individual assessments is to "weed out" the bad directors. This is simply not the case. With the increased focus on governance and the responsibilities and independence of the directors, most directors are diligent, come to meetings well prepared, and work hard on behalf of the shareholders they serve. The purpose of evaluations is simply to improve the performance of each director and thus the board. Therefore, for evaluations to be useful, they must be part of an overall evaluation process that is constructive and is built on the trust that exists amongst the directors.

An effective director evaluation process should have some structure, but it should also be relatively simple so that it does not consume more of the board's time than it should. A number of evaluation methods are evolving that can be considered. These include self-assessments, evaluations of board members conducted by the governance and nominating committee against a set of criteria, interviews by the chair or a lead director, or assessments facilitated by an outside person. Each board will need to consider what approach will work best for it.

However, if a board has not yet engaged in individual assessments, I would suggest that the best way to proceed is to acclimatize the directors by starting with the simple process of directors completing a self-assessment. This can be done by means of a straightforward written questionnaire that should include questions that will highlight what directors feel they contributed as well as what they feel they can do to improve their personal performance. Questions to help focus the review might include:

- What do you feel was your most significant contribution to the board's deliberations?
- Do you believe you participated effectively in board discussions and raised the tough questions in a constructive manner?
- What do you feel you need to do to enhance your effectiveness as a director?

Only after directors are comfortable with the initial process of self-evaluations will they be ready to advance to a more rigorous process, such as peer evaluations, one-on-one interviews, or an evaluation process conducted by an outside facilitator. This progression will take time and should not be rushed. Building an evaluation system that is based on trust among the directors is the key to ensuring that it will be successful in achieving the system's objectives.

I offer two remarks on what I think individual director assessments should *not* be. One—they should not be an annual and cumbersome process. Two—they should not be a ranking of directors against one another. Given that most boards meet only four to six times a year, with occasional additional meetings for specific items, doing assessments on an annual basis is probably not necessary. Once a process is in place and operating effectively, assessments can be done about every two years. Otherwise they tend to take up too much of the board's time with little benefit. I also do not believe a system that ranks one director against his or her peers adds value. Each director brings a unique set of skills and perspectives to the board and should be evaluated based on how well he or she is applying those skills and adding value to the board's deliberations. Ranking them from best to worst simply turns the process into a popularity contest and erodes the trust that directors have in one another.

CONCLUSION

To address effectively the issues relating to change of board composition, a board will likely want to consider:

- Reconceptualizing changes to board composition as positive and constructive;
- Obtaining consensus of the board and management on the level of engagement;
- Determining the right mix of hard and soft skills appropriate for the board in the circumstances and populating the board accordingly;
- Encouraging an open process for change to create a more self-actualizing board; and
- Considering different and creative sources from which to attract directors, such as an existing pool of seasoned business people who may be passed 'retirement age'.

To assess the performance of and grow a healthy board, you will want to:

- Implement board, board committee and director evaluation processes;
- Strategically socialize board, committee members and directors to these processes by starting with self-evaluation and ultimately moving to more objective forms of evaluation;
- Ensure the processes allow for constructive feedback and a mechanism to track implementation of that feedback;
- Be cautious that the processes not become too complex so as to defeat the purpose of the assessment; and
- Be careful not to pit director against director by engaging in ranking.

PART FIVE

EXECUTIVE COMPENSATION

Chapter 15
Senior Executive Compensation

THIS CHAPTER OFFERS a few observations on the ever-fashionable topic of senior executive compensation. Both theory and practice have changed quite a lot over the past few years as corporate fraud and failure have been traced in part to misguided and excessive compensation at or near the top.

Let me begin with a short reprise of some underlying and clarifying assumptions. My apologies for tilling what is old ground to some, though others either don't "get it" or don't accept its consequences.

- Greed is inherent in the human condition, though it's more evident in some sets of genes than in others. Greed is not without redeeming qualities (energy, achievement, wealth creation), but, for society's sake, it must be channelled and held within bounds.

- Knowledge is power. Management will always have more detailed and factual knowledge about their company, its operations, its prospects and plans than will its time-constrained independent directors. The power of deeper knowledge must be balanced and offset by the other powers that boards possess in law but have too often failed to use in practice.

- The combination of insufficiently controlled greed and power imbalance through superior knowledge leads to compensation excesses that in turn lead too often to short-term, overly opportunistic decisions, reckless over-expansion, rash acquisitions at inflated prices, fiddling the books, fraud, and the ultimate failure of bankruptcy. It's *The Rake's Progress* of Hogarth in a modern corporate setting.

And while these deeply unsettling breaches and flaws are hardly endemic, they are common enough and harmful enough to markets and to the free enterprise system that they require what I like to call "countervailing power" by boards of directors, although even that is not enough.

With this brief preamble, let me turn to best current practice—both process and substance—in widely held[1] public companies.

1. For public companies with both a control block and minority shareholders, it is general experience that representatives of that control block usually provide responsible oversight of executive compensation at the controlled-company level. It's usually in their own self-interest to do so. An exception might occur when a family member from the control block group is seconded to the management of the controlled company. In this situation, independent directors have both a special and an especially challenging responsibility to minority shareholders.

PROCESS

It seems to me that best practice includes, though may not be limited to, the following:

- The board comprises predominately competent and experienced independent directors. This is a necessary though insufficient component of good governance in general.

- The board chair and the CEO are two persons doing two very different jobs.

- The board, not management, is entirely responsible for board size, board and committee composition, and for both the selection of new and the retirement of existing directors.

- The compensation committee is composed entirely of independent directors.

- All members of the compensation committee are literate on compensation matters and, ideally, at least one is an expert. The analogy to the audit committee is obvious.

- Where literacy or expertise is lacking, director education about this and other crucial aspects of professional directorship in the twenty-first century is both needed and now available.

- The board and its compensation committee must be entirely free to hire, when useful, a compensation consultant of its choice. That consultant must then be responsible solely to the board committee and the full board.

- All aspects of the compensation of senior management are determined and controlled by the compensation committee and the full board.

- Management can either hire a separate compensation consultant for its own purposes or use the board's consultant, subject to the conditions stated above.

This choice involves a sensitive trade-off. Two sets of consultants likely mean higher costs as well as increased potential for conflict and working at cross-purposes. But the use of a single consultant raises the issue of where that consultant's primary loyalty lies. And since the retainer from management, especially in a large, multi-divisional, multi-site company is likely to be considerably larger than that from the compensation committee, the possibility of more aggressive recommendations for management compensation is an ongoing concern. However, I should add that the best consultants in this arena are acutely sensitive to this issue.

SUBSTANCE

SALARIES

On the reasonable assumption that additional pay for exceptional performance is best accomplished—principally—through variable compensation, base salaries for senior executives should be relatively modest. That is, they should be held to levels that can be justified across the full spectrum of the economic cycle and of consequent corporate performance. The alternative of cutting salaries when corporate performance is unacceptable may provide a useful, though harsh, object lesson, but it's neither normal nor best practice. Most people, even senior executives, come to depend on their salaries to cover their living expenses, present and planned.

The assumption that larger companies should pay higher executive compensation is deeply ingrained and, other things being equal, is reasonable. However, it is, I think, better for quite a lot of the higher compensation to be paid in one variable form or another.

Given a tough-minded but fair compensation committee of fully independent directors, what sort of salary guidelines make sense? Let's start with the self-evident assumption that this is definitely not an area where government regulation or even influence should play any part. Except in wartime, progressive taxation should be the limit of government involvement, and some object even to that.

The guideposts most commonly used for salary determination are peer-group comparisons facilitated by public-company disclosure and by consultants, some of whom have tended to use statistical magic to create the triumph of hope over experience by cramming 75 percent of CEOs into the top 25 percent of performers. The inevitable bootstrap effect follows. This triumph of greed over arithmetic reality—this spectacle of executive compensation increasingly divorced from superior economic performance—is hardly a shareholder-friendly face of capitalism.

Another approach, not used much in North America but somewhat more popular in Japan and parts of Western Europe, is to determine an appropriate relationship between the total direct compensation of a company's CEO and its lowest-paid, full-time employee after a year or two of service. The following illustrates the principle in a Canadian setting:

Company Size	*Total Cash Compensation Multiple*
Small-Cap (< $1 billion)	Up to 40
Mid-Cap ($1 - $3 billion)	Up to 60
Large-Cap (> $3 billion)	Up to 100

I chose the above multiples arbitrarily, and it's fair game, of course, to debate what they should be. Some CEOs will view the above numbers with distaste and even disdain. It's instructive to recall that, at the peak of the last economic boom that ended in 2000, the comparable multiple for the S&P 500 companies in the U.S. was about 450 and, for the largest 100 U.S. companies, was about 1000.

Regardless of the arithmetic, it seems to me that the principle of establishing some sort of compensation relationship between those at the top and those at the bottom of a company's pecking order is worth considering. Some will argue that it's corporate socialism in which those at the top of the pyramid are inhibited in their pursuit of as much wealth as they can accumulate. A better analogy, I think, is that, in the absence of inhibitions of one kind or another, there is a wealth transfer from shareholders to management. Warren Buffet called it, famously, the largest peacetime transfer of wealth in U.S. history. And shareholders have noticed.

Furthermore, at the societal level and speaking philosophically, a meritocratic democracy can evolve over time into a corporate plutocracy with perverse long-run consequences that we must guard against.

BONUSES

The enduring first principle is surely that there must be some clear relationship between the size of the bonus and both the quality of earnings and increases in those earnings. Of course, learned texts have been written on what to measure in establishing that critical link between bonus payments and performance, both corporate and individual.

The more senior the job, the more the bonus should be based on hard, bottom-line numbers. For CEOs, the great bulk of bonus payments should be so based. But not all. Steps to improve longer-run earnings usually have a short-run cost. Such steps should be bonusable and will involve both hard and soft data.

But most of the bonus for CEOs should relate to the last line on the income statement. As captain of the ship, the CEO is responsible for everything and must be held accountable and rewarded or not for all that transpires under his watch.

I recognize, of course, that arguments can be made in favour of a wide range of other hard numbers such as EVA, EBITDA, ROI, ROE, cash flow, and others limited only by the restless ingenuity of those who like to worry about these things. Personally, I subscribe to the reasoning behind Occam's Razor—that is, no more complex than necessary—or, in more contemporary jargon, KISS.

Another unending source of argument is the division of before-bonus profits between the senior executive group (as bonuses) and shareholders (as dividends or additions to retained earnings). The need to attract, retain, and motivate senior management must be balanced by board compensation committees against the immutable fact that shareholders own corporations and that returns to them via rising share prices and dividends are paramount. This is supported by shareholder theory,[2] by corporate jurisprudence, and by well-intentioned texts, homilies, and conventional wisdom.

In practice, to mangle the old Scottish proverb, "Who calls the tune, himself pays." That is, the greediness flaw that leads to out-of-line compensation has had its way too often with overly compliant and even supine boards.

So, again in practice and especially in future practice, it comes down to how boards are structured and how they function and whether they give deliberate and explicit weight to the trade-off between the best interests of shareholders and management groups. This is complicated by the fact that there's as much zero-sum involved as win-win.

Then there's the relationship between the bonus of the CEO and those of the rest of the executive group. There are enough variables in play that any rule of thumb must be advanced hesitantly but, as a rough generalization, the CEO is typically bonused at 1.5 to 2.5 times the amount awarded to the next most valued contributor. That's more descriptive than prescriptive, although the range is probably wide enough to serve prescription as well, except for a few outlier cases.

Options

While best practice today has moved rather sharply away from stock options for directors, it's not so clear-cut for executives.

2. Stakeholder theory, practised more in Western Europe than in North America, is a little unclear on returns to senior executives versus shareholders.

It's true that a few companies have moved to eliminate options altogether, but most continue to feel that they are a useful weapon in the compensation arsenal if—and this is pivotal—a few important conditions are established and met.

- First, performance options should be used much more than they are. They should, in fact, become the norm. In a strong bull market, too many senior executives took home unconscionable amounts of money principally because price-earning ratios rose dramatically, mainly because the demand for stocks rose in relation to their supply, and that was largely because the huge baby boomer cohort was entering the major savings phase of its members' life cycle.[3]

  Performance options pay off generously only when there is superior performance, that is, when pre-determined stretch targets are met or exceeded. These targets can be any combination of internal absolute or external absolute or external relative measures. That the use of performance options has been and continues to be restrained—an understatement—is again testimony to the muted role of boards in taking tougher stands on compensation issues in general.

- Another aspect of best practice is to insist that shares acquired through options be held for not less than a year and preferably two years. An exception can be made, upon request, for an executive to sell enough shares to cover the cost of exercise

3. The first baby boomers were born in 1946. By 1990, they were 44 years old. That's about when mortgages are paid off, second homes are bought, and there is a growing awareness that retirement is only a couple of decades away ... or less. Time to start planning for it. The last baby boomers were born in 1964. They turn 44 in 2008. The game is still afoot.

and related tax. Why "upon request"? Because executives—certainly those at or near the top of an organization—are paid well enough to handle these option-related costs out of savings, except in unusual circumstances. In any event, shares acquired by option exercise should be held long enough to minimize the possibility or even the appearance of selling on bad news that has not yet reached the public domain.

- This leads to the related point that all senior executives should hold, for as long as employed, company shares in the amount of not less than three to seven times annual salary. The more senior the position, the greater the multiple.[4] Share acquired through option exercise provide one excellent way to help meet this requirement.

- A word or two about option vesting and term. Vesting at twenty percent per year over five years is fairly common and is, in my view, best practice. Certainly full vesting at time of grant is unwise. It's better practice to spread over a longer period the incentives that an option provides.

  On term, I'm somewhat ambivalent. I've noticed a movement recently to shorten term from, typically, ten to seven or even to five years. If it's usual at end of term simply to re-grant the same number of options or even more, I'm not sure that term-shortening accomplishes much, although the grantee does pay the company earlier for exercising the original grant. Furthermore, if the re-grant is done selectively, thoughtfully, and judicially, a shorter term means an earlier

4. In a press release of December 18, 2003, TD Bank president and CEO Ed Clark said he would be required to own five to ten times his salary in shares of his bank.

decision on any new grant and sends a useful signal sooner to the original option-holder.

On the other hand, longer-term options ought to encourage a longer-term perspective. In recent years, we've had more than our share of short-term thinking.

- Finally, options should be expensed. The tedious, though important, debate about how best to do it has come to an end, at least in Canada.[5] Beginning in fiscal 2004, Canadian corporations no longer have a choice; the expensing of options is mandated. This will almost surely have a moderating effect on some of the more outrageous levels of options granted in recent years. This does not, however, lessen the need for a strong, independent compensation committee and board as gatekeepers or adjudicators between the best interests of shareholders and executives.[6]

PENSIONS AND PERQUISITES

To start with, it's clear that the investing public would be better served by more open disclosure. Pension arrangements for senior executives have been dubbed "stealth compensation," a legitimate criticism that has helped to bring light to some shady nooks and crannies, though more needs to be done. But as a result of media and institutional investor pressures, the process of public enlightenment has begun.

5. Late bulletin. After years of acrimonius debate, there is now grudging agreement in the U.S. that options will be expensed for fiscal periods beginning June 15, 2005, and later.
6. Some argue that recent Canadian experience with excessive executive compensation and related chicanery has, on the whole, been less harmful than that in the U.S. Perhaps. But the two economies have enough in common that undue comfort should not be taken. Nor should we assume that future experience will necessarily replicate the past.

In April 2005, for example, the *New York Times* listed several of the largest pension entitlements of retired senior executives, primarily former CEOs, in the U.S. Their pensions range between three and six million dollars per year. The annual pensions of a couple of recently retired Canadian bank CEOs are near the bottom of this range. Such numbers are surprisingly generous and it is certainly desirable that pension grants at and near the top of a corporation be in the public domain.

A widely used device to increase pensions for senior executives hired away from other companies, when pensions are not transferable, is to credit two or more years of service for every year of actual service or, alternatively, to add anywhere from five to as many as twenty years of service arbitrarily. Either way, the result is to increase the ultimate pension by amounts that can be very considerable.

It is, of course, a competitive world out there for the most talented executives, although the actual talent pool is probably larger than generally believed by managements and their consultants.

Certainly it is not surprising that executives hired from the outside, mostly in their forties to fifties—middle to late-middle age—are as concerned about their security in retirement as they are about their more immediate employment income. Full disclosure of this tactic of increasing arbitrarily years of service is an essential component of fuller disclosure of all pension arrangements for at least the top five executives in a company.

A word or two about retirement benefits beyond pensions is in order. The classic example of a former star CEO "outed" in this matter was Jack Welch, who did such a splendid job for GE shareholders over many years of strong leadership. The details of his benefits in retirement became public only because of a rather adversarial—and public—divorce settlement.

His stellar, almost iconic, reputation was sullied at least a little by the disclosure, certainly not intended by GE, of such perks as the use of private jets, hotel suites, apartments, daily flowers, and theatre tickets.

It seems to me that, for CEOs and other senior executives, the combination of lifetime earnings (salaries, bonuses, stock and option grants, retiring allowances) and generous pensions makes it unnecessary and unseemly to tack on a long list of additional benefits through retirement.

The impression conveyed is one of greed and pettiness and hanging on to the trappings of former status. Surely this image outweighs the benefits, usually marginal in relation to the pension itself and to net worth, provided to the retired business leader. Certainly it does not enhance reputations, either personal or corporate.

I'd like now to comment briefly on the miscellany of other perks that need not be detailed under U.S. regulations if they cost in total less than $50,000 per executive per year. They include such common benefits as cars, clubs of various kinds, travel, and entertainment such as boxes or seats at major sports or cultural events.[7]

7. One of the audit technique guides (ATGs) of the IRS is entitled Fringe Benefits ATG. It provides a more complete list, a veritable cornucopia of overflowing bensions. Here it is, in all its splendour: "Athletic Skyboxes/Cultural Entertainment Suites, Awards/Bonuses, Club Memberships, Corporate Credit Cards, Executive Dining Rooms, Loans, Outplacement Services, Qualified Employee Discounts, Security-related Transportation, Spousal/Dependent Life Insurance, Transportation, Chauffeurs, Employer-paid Parking, Transfer of Property, Employee Use of Listed Property, Relocation Expenses, Non-commercial Air Travel, Employer-paid Vacations, Spousal or Dependent Travel, Wealth Management, Qualified Retirement Planning, and Employer-paid FICA Taxes."

Almost invariably, the business benefit and the personal benefit are so intertwined that separation is a labyrinth of complexity and, though required, scarcely worth the effort. Regardless, many corporations bend over backwards to keep their CEOs—and others near the top—cheerful and contented and perhaps even motivated.

For the most part, I take a fairly relaxed view of this sub-category of executive compensation. Obviously the worst excesses need to be publicized and excised. Rolls-Royces, Ferraris and Aston Martins should not be on the corporate dispensary. Nor, to the extent that they create tax deductions, should they be a claim on the public purse and partly paid for by you and me.

Similarly, entrance fees and annual dues for some rarefied clubs should be made public and questioned. I'm talking about very high-end clubs with an entry fee of $350,000 to $500,000 (occasionally, even higher) along with annual dues of $50,000 to $75,000 (occasionally even higher).

But, except for these sorts of way-over-the-top expenses, this broad category of executive benefit is not as abused as direct compensation and pension benefits.

AN AFTERTHOUGHT

When I think, as I sometimes do, about executive compensation in the context of secular change over the past, say, fifty years, I conclude that a maturation process has been slowly evolving. And it seems to me that, broadly, this process has involved four successive phases of which the fourth is still only incipient.

In the first phase, executive compensation was largely handled in a highly confidentia, even secretive and furtive, way. When I joined a division of Union Carbide (now part of Dow

Chemical) some half-century ago, I had not the faintest idea of what anybody earned, from the CEO on down to my fellow new-graduate recruits.

You'll remember, perhaps, an old joke from that era. An executive hands a sealed envelope to his younger subordinate and says, "You've done a good job for us, Wilson, so this informs you of a salary increase. But I caution you to keep this matter totally confidential." The subordinate opens the envelope, scans its contents, and says, "Right, sir. I won't tell a soul. I'm as ashamed of it as you are."

In any event, to the extent that any senior executive compensation did become public in those days, the prevailing reaction was generally more approving than disapproving. Perhaps upward mobility and the Horatio Alger legend were more alive and well then than now. And perhaps the media—a cynical and envious group, taken as a whole—have hardened hearts (both their own and those of their audiences), even as they have become more powerful. And finally, a point I try to make a little later in this chapter, senior executive compensation in those days was a much smaller multiple of that earned by the typical office or factory worker.

In Canada, the second phase began with the decision of the Rae government in Ontario (1990–1995) to mandate disclosure of compensation for the five most highly-paid executives. Over the next several years, the result, perversely enough, was to set off a competitive game in which, first, executives of competing companies in the same industry, but, later, executives as a class did their best to ensure that they were at or near the top of their "comparables" and certainly above the median, creating that well-known, infamous ratcheting effect.

Then came Enron, Tycos, WorldCom—name your own favourite corporate disaster—and a rapidly growing recognition, spurred on by the media and by others motivated by either envy or Robin Hood–ism, that compensation and performance were too often unrelated.

Thus the third of the four phases embraced the mantra "Pay for performance." And so people like Jack Welch, who was very well paid on his watch, were regarded benignly, while people like Carly Fiorina or Michael Eisner, who were also very well paid but delivered much poorer results to shareholders, were criticized roundly and regarded in some circles as corporate liabilities.

Personally, I think the "Pay for performance" approach is basically sound, if planned and executed with care and rigour, not always the norm. In fact, the worst kind of compensation practice is to talk the right game but walk a different one. Too often, bonuses, share grants, and options have been instruments in perpetuating a myth that exceptional performance is necessary to earn them. In reality, total direct compensation has often been understood to materialize at some agreed level, largely regardless of the rhetoric.

In essence, variable compensation has been treated in result, though not in form, like fixed compensation. That there must be an unequivocal link with performance has been viewed by some managements, unencumbered by a strong, independent board, as an amiable, consensual fiction. That this has become somewhat less common recently is encouraging, though largely attributable to stronger external pressures.

But I now see a fourth phase growing in strength and emboldened by the seemingly interminable litany of companies "gone wrong" for any one or more of the several well-known reasons cited throughout this book. This fourth phase can be captured in two sentences. That is, regardless of performance, executive compensation has grown rapidly over the past couple of decades in relation to gross national product, compensation more broadly, and even return to shareholders. And this has not gone unnoticed.

Perhaps the most telling corroborating statistic is the well-quoted observation that, from 1988 to 2001, S&P CEO direct compensation (not including pensions and various fringe benefits) rose from 40 to 450 times that of the lowest-paid full-time employee, though this ratio has fallen off a little since then.

If phase four of the four phases that I've briefly described gathers in strength and momentum, new and rather unfamiliar issues will confront boards and compensation committees. It's somewhat ironic that public sector conviction that broader disclosure of senior executive compensation would exercise a moderating influence may finally be affirmed, despite its earlier influence to the contrary.

Chapter 16

Stock Options I: Improve Their Utility or Abandon Them

SOME TIME AGO, William (Bill) Miller, the esteemed investment savant at Legg Mason of Baltimore, advocated the abolition of executive stock options. His views received wide publicity and, while they are thoughtful and reasonable, abolition is, I believe, a more draconian remedy than is warranted.

I do agree with Mr. Miller that outright share ownership comes closer than any other form of executive compensation to aligning management and shareholder interests. That is, share ownership provides both the upside potential for gain and the downside risk of loss that put management and shareholders in precisely the same position.

The problem, however, is that ownership is limited in many individual cases by the personal resources needed by executives to fund share purchases. And even if a company has an investment loan program,[1] ownership levels continue to be limited both by the cost of servicing such loans and, more important, by the level of risk that executives are willing to (or should) assume. These costs and risks often become problems at levels below those where the financial incentives from share ownership are great enough to make a sufficient motivational difference.

Because options require no upfront cash from executives, they provide added leverage, more bang for the buck. In other words, because there's no cash downside for the recipient and no cash outlay for the grantor, option grants can be larger than is practical for share grants.[2] But this cannot be said more strongly: the desired upper level of grant stops far short of the ridiculous and abusive number of options granted all too frequently over the past decade.

The problem with options lies not in the principle but in the practice. That is, the problem is not with the inherent characteristics of options but with both the excessive number of options granted and the often inadequate linkages to economic performance. Let us not throw out the darling baby with the eminently expendable bath water.

There are four remedial actions needed to make the use of executive options more palatable to investors, influential commentators, and the public.

First, the value of options granted needs to be limited and controlled by a board compensation committee solely comprising

1. In some plans, the dividend paid on the shares reverts to the company and is deemed to be the interest owed, but there are usually tax consequences for the shareholder.
2. This assumes that the shares needed to support exercise come from treasury and are not purchased in the marketplace. The former is by far the most common source.

fully independent and diligent directors. It should be advised, as necessary, by an external consultant totally separate from any hired by management to advise management. In some cases, CEOs have been almost free to write their own tickets, supported by a supine board of directors.

As a rough rule of thumb, the net present value of an option grant, when allocated to each year of its term, should rarely, if ever, exceed the salary of the recipient. This rule has, of course, been widely ignored, often to foolish extremes. Everyone can cite a horror story or two about wildly excessive grants.

The situation is further worsened by some statistical evidence that the Black–Scholes formula widely used to price executive options undervalues them systematically by a considerable amount. This causes too many options to be granted to produce a given targeted net present value. This is not, incidentally, a criticism of Messrs. Black & Scholes who developed their valuation model for an entirely different kind of short-term option.

Second, performance options should become the norm, not the uncommon exception. Options should pay out if and only if corporate performance is demonstrably superior, measured in absolute or relative terms or both. This sensible approach will be discussed more fully in the next chapter.

Third, the cost to a company of options granted should be expensed. While it's obviously important not to count the cost twice (the cost of dilution through the issue of treasury shares to satisfy option exercise is already being borne), the fact that there's no expense recorded on an income statement is clearly misleading. The expensing of options is now mandatory in Canada. In the U.S., vested interests fought hard for as little expensing and as favourable a method as possible. But, as noted in the previous chapter, option expensing will commence for fiscal periods beginning June 15th of 2005 and later. An obvious and benign side effect of expensing options, at least from a shareholder perspective, is that simple economics will militate against some of the more egregious examples of excessive grants. A hit to the bottom line always sobers the mind.

Fourth, there need to be tougher rules about how long shares acquired through option exercise should be held. Whether the necessary changes should be mandated by government regulation or left to individual boards of directors is open to debate. I prefer the latter but the former may be necessary by default. Regardless of the means, the short-term sale of shares acquired through option exercise must be discouraged. Similarly, the long-term hold of such shares must be encouraged. The sale of enough shares to pay for the cost of exercise should, if requested, be permitted.

An appropriate combination of carrot and stick might include a higher capital gains tax on shares held for less than, say, two years. That's the stick. The carrot might be the sharp reduction or even elimination of capital gains tax on shares held for longer than two years. The longer I think about it, the more I am convinced that these changes in tax policy would have a serious impact on the "short-termism" that has led to irrational decision-making and absurd market swings. Such changes would also, of course, inhibit exercising options and jumping ship in advance of bad news.

Sadly, tax changes like this do not take place quickly or without debate *ad nauseam*. With such tax changes, no further regulatory action or board decision would be necessary.

Without them, the carrot is absent and the stick would, as I said, need to be replaced by either government regulations affecting all boards or individual board policy accompanied by mandatory public disclosure.

With the above four areas of change in place, I submit that most of the well-founded criticism of options as a component of executive compensation would largely disappear. From the perspective of investors and shareholders, options would continue to provide essentially the same motivational advantage which they have traditionally provided but without the baggage of those glaringly obvious weaknesses that, along with other issues, have poisoned the well of investor confidence.

Chapter 17

Stock Options II: Performance Options

I START FROM the premise articulated in the previous chapter that options should continue to be an integral part of senior executive compensation. Companies like them because there is no cash cost, so long as the shares needed to permit exercise are from treasury, as is usual, instead of acquired in the market. Companies like them even more, of course, when there is no requirement to expense them and this is why the U.S. corporate community fought so strenuously in a rearguard action to delay expensing and to do it in as benign, if misleading, way as possible.

Individual executives like options because they are taxed at capital gains rates, now roughly half the rate applied to salaries and bonuses. And, with recent changes in tax law, capital gains tax is deferred[1] and applied, not when options are exercised, but when shares acquired are sold.

1. In Canada, the deferral is limited to a maximum of $100K per year.

Investors like options in principle (though not always in application) because they seemed to come closer than other forms of compensation to integrating the objectives and best interests of shareholders and management. True, there is potential dilution in earnings per share. But this is avoided if awarded options create enough additional incentive to cause earnings to grow by a greater percentage than additional shares issued. Granted, this cause and effect relationship can never be proven. More recently, there have been some concerns raised about the overemphasis that some option plans place on goals that put too much weight on the short term.

If, on balance, options are desirable in principle, performance options are better still, at least from an investor perspective. They demand more in executive performance than share prices rising in a broad bull market. In a market such as we experienced through most of the nineties, price-earnings ratios grew for reasons having less to do with corporate performance than with external (exogenous) factors. One such factor has been and still is baby boomers in a strong savings phase of their lives and with few, if any, other investment opportunities yielding as good a long-run performance as equities.[2]

In short, the old saw that a "rising tide lifts all boats" suggests that options should pay off as richly as was common in the nineties only when performance is better than that delivered by the market as a whole. In this context, performance should be measured by some mix of absolute internal criteria

2. Real estate comes close, especially at the date of writing, in the later stages of a long, strong upcycle. This current real estate boom in most of the western world has been as sturdy as an oak but no tree grows to the sky! This applies, of course, to all investments, including equities, as can be ruefully attested to by the tech boom of the nineties.

and relative external criteria. The following chart illustrates this principle:

Performance Hurdles

	Internal Operational Measures	*External Stock Market Measures*
Absolute Hurdle(s)	Must achieve some financial goal, such as return on equity or on investment.	Must achieve some agreed percent increase in share price.
Relative Hurdle(s)	Must exceed, by an agreed percentage, a comparable measure (such as ROE or ROI) achieved by an appropriate peer group.	Must exceed, by some agreed percentage, the share price increase achieved by an appropriate peer group.

If the selected hurdle(s) is met, exercise is triggered, subject, of course, to vesting and term provisions. And the strike price is the market price at time of grant. With performance options, the vesting period is usually determined by the period over which performance is measured. Ideally, this should be anywhere from three to seven years or even longer. With longer periods, there can be partial vesting for reaching pre-determined intermediate or milestone performance levels.

There's also a harsher model in which the strike price is the market price at the time the selected hurdle(s) is met. This model is uncommon, even within the uncommoness of performance options more generally. It strikes most observers as unfair. In addition, it provides additional psychological incentives for executives to argue for lower hurdles.

To sum up, a major trend over the past couple of decades has been the rise of options as a central and even dominant component of executive compensation, relative to salaries and bonuses, for reasons that I have described. Furthermore, despite the temporary damping effect of cyclical down-markets on option payouts, it seems highly likely that the trend will continue.

However, because options often deliver large rewards for average results (in relation to investor expectations and peer group performance, or both), a strong case can be made, as argued here, that performance options should be used more frequently. Compensation consultants and board compensation committees should give this instrument much more weight than they have to date. These bodies and boards generally must take the initiative. Certainly it is unreasonable to expect many managements to lead the charge and push enthusiastically for more demanding and potentially less rewarding forms of incentive compensation than those to which they have become accustomed.

Finally, let me mention a variation on the performance option theme which is, I believe, underutilized. I refer to extending their use to include grants for individualized performance at levels below the CEO. There is, of course, nothing unusual about rewarding local-level performance with corporate-level instruments, that is, stock options or grants. What is unusual is tying the release of options for exercise and award directly to specific local-level performance hurdles.

Here are two hypothetical examples:

- In a functional organization, the senior sales and marketing person and the senior manufacturing and operations person might each be granted options exercisable only if gross margin increases by some agreed amount, whether in absolute dollars, in percentage terms and/or as a percent of revenue.

- In a conglomerate or a divisionalized company, the subsidiary president or divisional general manager might be granted options exercisable only if bottom line performance of that person's operational responsibilities rises to some agreed level and/or by some agreed percentage.

This extension of performance options is, of course, where bonuses have been traditionally used. It is crucial that only easily measured, unambiguous performance objectives be used. "Soft" goals are open to interpretation and, therefore, disagreement, both in design and in measurement.

To conclude, not only are performance options underemployed in general but their potential use can be modestly extended to reward superior performance, measured unambiguously in quantitatively demanding terms, of senior line executives below the CEO and other corporate-level executives.

Chapter 18

Stock Options III: Directors in the Middle

RECENTLY I PARTICIPATED in a panel discussion on stock options hosted by William M. Mercer. Each of the four panelists represented a different constituency: management, the board of directors, the institutional investor, and the compensation consultant. As could be predicted, the perspectives offered were significantly, even profoundly, different, and reflected the broad self-interest of each constituency.

I believe that the independent director is more likely to hold a relatively unbiased, middle-of-the road position on executive options than the other three constituencies. As the old saw puts it, where you stand depends on where you sit. And the independent director sits midway between management and shareholders and mediates between these two groups in situations where their respective interests diverge. Compensation in general, options in particular, is one such area.

This mediation role is especially important in a widely held company where there is no control block. Where there is one, the controlling shareholder(s) almost always wields effective control of compensation, and indeed of all issues of any consequence. In a widely held company, this mediation role is played far more effectively when the chairman and CEO are two different people and when the former is a truly independent director and not, for example, the previous CEO.

Even when the roles are separated and the chairman is well and truly independent, it is all too easy for a board to be co-opted on compensation issues and to align itself more with management than with the shareholder. Or as Mark Twain once famously and rather cynically said, "If anyone says 'It's not the money, it's the principle of the thing'—it's the money."

Why is co-option possible, even likely? Here are three reasons:

- Some board members are still beholden to a company's CEO for their appointments. This is not as common as it was a decade or more ago but clearly it still happens and perhaps more often than meets the eye, especially in mid-size and smaller companies.

- The majority of directors, especially of larger companies, are still CEOs or retired CEOs. And so there is a natural community of interest and broad identification with management's mindset and aspirations.

- Most boards are still advised on compensation issues by the same consultant hired by management. This is not universally

> true: some boards recognize the obvious potential for conflict and hire a separate consultant. But it is true often enough to raise concerns. Consultants are usually honest folk and sensitive to conflict-of-interest issues, but they nevertheless find it difficult, I submit, not to remember who hires them and pays their bills.

On management compensation questions in general and on options in particular, even the fairest and most informed directors face a familiar, indeed classic, dilemma. On the one hand, there is and always will be a shortage of true and lasting leaders. And, as with star athletes or movie stars, competition for the very good, let alone the best, is intense.

On the other hand, we can all cite nefarious examples of excessive compensation, some more widely known and infamous than others. Numbers of dollars that were unheard of a generation or even a decade ago are too often being paid today for corporate performance that is mediocre at best. It's the juxtaposition of egregious compensation levels and sub-par performance that makes shareholders see red.

No shareholder should object to options that pay off if and only if a company outperforms its peers in its field or in as closely related a field as can be identified. Superior performance can be measured by relative stock price gains over a sustained period or by one or more relative internal measures like ROI or ROE or by a mix of external and internal criteria. One reason performance options have not been used much is that, in the U.S., they had to be expensed, unlike regular options historically and until new regulations are finally in place. This gives new meaning to the word "dysfunctional."

It is retilling old ground to say that the accounting treatment of options has been an international disgrace. To quote that outspoken critic of option excesses, Warren Buffett:

> Accounting principles offer management a choice: pay employees in one form and count the cost, or pay them in another form and ignore the cost. Small wonder then that the use of options has mushroomed. … If options aren't a form of compensation, what are they? If compensation isn't an expense, what is it? And if expenses shouldn't go into the calculation of earnings, where in the world should they go?

The principal reason that change-in-option accounting has been so long in coming is, of course, that if options are treated as the expense that they are, the negative impact on corporate earnings and therefore on share prices will, in some instances, be severe. A related reason is that expensed options will surely be issued more parsimoniously than options that do not affect the income statement. Options have created far more multimillionaires than all other forms of executive compensation lumped together.

Earnings repercussions and disgruntled executives accustomed to historically larger option grants make it clear that the expensing of options is not a win-win scenario. Nevertheless, it's the right thing to do and will, among other things, help to restore some sanity to excessive, in some cases wildly excessive, grants that have almost become the norm for the CEOs of most large, widely held companies in the U.S. and, to a lesser degree, elsewhere.

Finally, there's the issue of option re-pricing, a topic that makes the news from time to time when companies re-price to retain mid-level managers who could, in effect, re-price for themselves by walking to a competitor. This creates a dilemma with horns, if ever there was one.

In general and on principle, I find the re-pricing of options to be repugnant. The central argument against the practice lies at the heart of the integrity of shareholder capitalism. It's not a complex or sophisticated argument. It's simply that, if a CEO receives options at $30 per share and the stock price drops over, say, a year to $15 and those options are then re-priced (even if cut back in number to provide the same net present value as before), that CEO is getting a second chance. If the stock then recovers over, say, another year, that CEO has a pre-tax gain of $15 per option re-priced. By contrast, the shareholder who bought at $30 per share only breaks even if the stock recovers to $30. He or she didn't get that second chance.

On the other hand, we all know that certain industries, notably high-tech, try to pay largely in options because they can't afford to pay much in cash. And in the kind of cyclical world in which many high-tech companies, large and small, operate, option re-pricing helps to prevent wholesale defections from one survivor organization to another.

Clearly the pressures to resort to re-pricing are real and large. Nevertheless, other less controversial ways[1] to hold key employees must be found. The sense of unfairness on the part of investors, both institutional and personal, is palpable and it will neither lessen nor go away.

1. One tool that can help in some cases is performance-related stock grants.

PART SIX
OBSERVATIONS ON SEVERAL CURRENTLY USEFUL TOPICS

Chapter 19

A Cautionary Tale: A Case Study of Director Risk

GENERAL BACKGROUND

Through fifty-five corporate boards over forty-two years, I have sat on fourteen where the company has been acquired or merged, mostly but not all via friendly takeovers. And I have sat on three where a company has suffered the ignominy of bankruptcy. The first two of these three were described in my 2002 book, *Excellence in the Boardroom*.

Silcorp Limited was the classic case of a business where the second-generation patriarch of a founding family found it difficult to make the transition to professional manager and CEO of a fairly large public company. After ill-advised expansion into the eastern U.S. and a reluctance to adopt a strategy of restructuring and cost containment, the company failed to meet some bond payments and went into CCAA, the rough and not quite as redemptive equivalent of Chapter 11 in the U.S.[1] There it remained for nearly a year.

It emerged with a new strategy, new management, and a partly reconstituted board. The shares were re-listed at $2 a share. Six years later, the company was sold in a friendly transaction to Couche-Tard of Québec for $46 a share, after adjusting for a stock split. A happy ending.

The second case was Interlink Freight Systems. This was the venerable CP Express and Transport sold by CP Rail in 1994 to its 3000 employees. Management held 10 percent, the non-unionized employees held 20 percent, and the union employees held 70 percent in a trust voted by the Transportation and Communications Union.

The board was made up of five independents, three members of management, and three union representatives. This made it difficult to reach consensus on matters such as the badly needed cost–cutting that became imperative after NAFTA, when the pattern of shipments shifted appreciably to north–south. As a consequence, competition from non-unionized U.S. carriers intensified. Furthermore, the company was under-financed; CP Rail had been tough-minded in the financial structure that it transferred to Interlink. The perhaps inevitable outcome was CCAA and the company did not survive. Not a happy ending.

PARTICULAR BACKGROUND

The third case is now in litigation and I shall describe briefly the circumstances but without names.

1. Chapter 11 in the U.S. and CCAA in Canada are designed to help companies get back on their feet again. Chapter 7 in the U.S. leads inevitably to bankruptcy and dissolution.

I joined this public–company board as a fully independent, outside director in 1997. The chairman was a former U.S. state governor. I joined shortly after another Canadian, a respected CEO, joined, and at the same time as a former premier of a Canadian province.

The company provided diversified services: construction, management, maintenance, and environment remediation in the refining, petrochemical, utility, and forest products industries.

Although the company was incorporated in Ontario, senior management, via a wholly owned subsidiary holding company incorporated in Delaware, was mostly located in a large southern U.S. city. Sometime later, a small head office was established in Toronto, after the chairmanship shifted to a Canadian.

The CEO was a likeable, amiable man, but I came to realize gradually that the combination of his experience and judgment was not up to the task of leading a heterogeneous, geographically diverse, complex set of businesses and subsidiaries in a rough-and-tumble, competitive industry.

Nevertheless, in the heady nineties, the company grew and seemed to prosper. The share price rose considerably over the first couple of years of my directorship. Compensation included stock options, and all directors at one point had a substantial capital gain. Although there was no vesting period, I felt, as a relatively new director, that it would be inappropriate to exercise and sell shares so early in the game. So I didn't.

In early 1998, a proposition surfaced to acquire a fairly large Canadian company that was partly in the same general line of work. At a pivotal board meeting, this acquisition was debated vigorously for several hours. Opinion was divided. Of the seven directors, two or three were outspokenly negative, including me. One concern was the rather unsavoury reputation of some of the owner-principals. Others, however, saw turnaround potential and an opportunity for significant growth.

In the event, a decision was made to acquire. One director, who had been strongly opposed, resigned shortly thereafter. I did not, following my long-held principle that directors are needed most when the seas roughen. The decision to acquire turned out to be a very bad one. Although the acquisition never did take place, the decision initiated an adverse chain of events, including a substantial down payment to the principals of the other company, that led, some two years later, to Chapter 11 in the U.S. and to CCAA in Canada. I resigned shortly thereafter; the other directors remained until the company when into Chapter 7 and expired, not very much later.

In the autumn of 2001, former directors and management received notice of a "plaintiff's original petition": a threatened lawsuit with a trial demanded. It referred to "ill-fated and fraudulent investments" along with charges of serious mismanagement.

After seeking legal advice, I wrote at the time to lawyers for the plaintiff (a consortium of bondholders). I stated clearly that, while I had held and expressed concerns about the capacity of management, I saw absolutely and categorically nothing at board level that even hinted at "unethical" or "fraudulent."

In June 2004, more than two and a half years later, directors and management were served with a lawsuit. The case will be heard in the same southern U.S. state where operating management had been located. The three independent Canadian directors have retained U.S. counsel to respond preliminarily to the suit and to act for us throughout. U.S. directors have also retained counsel in two or three law firms.

A little more relevant background. It is useful to remember that this storyline took place in the blander, more forgiving environment that could be dubbed pre-Enron (and prior to a great host of subsequent debacles). For example, the board met once a quarter, about half of the time in the U.S., half in Canada. Occasionally a short telephonic board meeting was called. There were board committees that met irregularly and briefly.

There were many topics where the board was either not involved at all, strikingly under-involved, or informed in a highly sanitized and watered-down way. Many relevant, even important, aspects of many issues and themes were never brought to the board's attention.

There are, I think, a few useful lessons for directors that can be distilled from this dreary tale. But let me first recapitulate briefly. Four points should be noted:

- While there was certainly a directors and officers ("D&O") insurance policy in place, lawyers for the carrier wrote a standard risk-avoidance letter that attempted in considerable detail to minimize or eliminate obligations of the insurer to the insured. (Subsequently, the carrier did accept the responsibility to defend both officers and directors.)

- All defendants must, of course, respond to the lawsuit within a reasonable time frame. Until the D&O issue was resolved, legal expenses (in U.S. dollars) were borne by those being sued. (This too has since been resolved satisfactorily.)

- The case will be tried in a district court of a southern U.S. state.

- Tough questions will surely be asked. Did directors pay sufficient attention to their duties and responsibilities? Was the "prudent man" standard always met? Obviously, I think so but, more important, what will a U.S. court decide about Canadian directors (and others, of course) involved in various ways with a company that failed? Naturally, many factors were at work. These included a highly competitive external environment, witnessed by the fact that other companies in the same line of business also failed a little later.

LESSONS LEARNED

Every experience, good and bad, provides an opportunity for learning, without which George Santayana's oft-quoted observation is apt: "Those who cannot remember the past are condemned to repeat it." The lessons that follow are hardly original but it is still useful to reiterate them here in the interests of good governance.

1. D&O policies are invariably written in legalese. Take legal advice to inform you fully (in the fullest sense of "fully") about the policy in place for each board on which you sit.

    - What's excluded?

    - Who assumes the up-front defence costs?

    - What is the carrier's responsibility for legal fees when the interests of the sued parties are or may be several and divergent?

- Is the maximum coverage adequate for the range of potential risks?

- Is there a "Pacman" clause that reduces coverage by the cost of legal fees?

- What is the reputation and track record of the carrier?

Good D&O policies are more expensive than ever but, in an increasingly litigious world, they are indispensable.

2. During the nineties, I sat on about a dozen corporate boards at any one time. During the eighties, the number was even larger. In the comparatively benign pre-Enron era, that was not uncommon, although hindsight suggests that was a heavy load to carry. In today's more demanding environment, even five may be too many, depending on the mix and on what other activities concern and distract you.

   If there is one clear lesson that flows from the sad recital of recent corporate misadventures in every industrialized country and business sector, it is the self-evident reality that boards demand the full attention of every director for far more hours than have been needed before.

3. Should you decide to disagree with a board decision, not only should you speak up but you should ensure that your dissent is properly recorded. In the ever more likely event of a lawsuit of one kind or another, a dissent against a decision that is dubious (or even against a decision that, given all the

facts, is defensible but the eventual outcome is dubious or worse) can be very important indeed.

It is sad but true that the concept of "cabinet solidarity" on important decisions is weakened by the threat of lawsuits directed against directors. To protect corporate and director interests, board minutes traditionally and almost invariably have been anodyne and couched in soft generalities. This is a double-edged sword and may, in future, be influenced by individual directors insisting on more disclosure of their views and votes on controversial decisions.

4. Keep copious private notes for future use, if and when necessary. Explain to yourself candidly, fully, and, of course, honestly, your support or otherwise for key policies and decisions. Work on the assumption that such notes may be needed in the event that a lawsuit is ever filed against you. I cannot say that I recommend this step without distaste, but we live in a very different world today than the one in which I served most of my years as a director.

5. When you, as a director, view a board decision as too risky or even reckless, you must, of course, say so. But, even more important, you should resign if the decision is board approved and if your concerns are deep-seated enough and if no other effective recourse appears to be available. You should also resign if you have lost confidence in some mix of the CEO, the board chairman and/or the board collectively, and if you become convinced that you cannot bring about any meaningful change by staying.

As noted earlier, I have always lived by the belief that directors should hang in there in troubled times on the assumption that that's when directors are needed most and that's when the you-know-whats desert a ship in danger of sinking. But I am now coming around reluctantly to the view that, while hanging in there loyally and resolutely may be the honourable thing to do, it is also quixotic and potentially inimical to one's net reputation and worth.

6. On the more specific issue of audit committees, accept appointments only under these assumptions:

   - You're fully prepared to dedicate a great deal more time than was typical in the pre–SARBOX, pre–new OSC regulations era. Count on a time multiple of three or more.

   - You are fully literate. And you, in your own heart, are as good judge of this as whether or not you seem to conform to some formal regulatory standard.

   - At least one member of every audit committee should be an "expert," though not necessarily the chair. For liability reasons, no one should be labelled an expert unless required, as in the U.S. under NYSE and NASDAQ rules. In Canada, there is no "expert" requirement except for companies interlisted on one of these U.S. exchanges. In the governance world of today and looking forward, it is more likely than ever before that professional acountants will migrate to this role. Certainly others meet this higher test but perhaps not as many as think they do.

CONCLUSION

In the brave new world of directorship in this young century, the risk/reward balance has shifted adversely. Directors today are exposed to much greater risks that can easily dwarf recent increases in director compensation. Has the pendulum swung too far? Many directors think so. Many investors and others do not. Time will tell.

Finally, it is crucial to distinguish between corporate failure caused by some variant of fraud—manipulation of the books, treating corporate assets like a personal piggy bank, wildly excessive and totally unjustified compensation, outright theft—and failure caused by the ebb and flow of fortunes in some hyper-competitive industry in a mostly Darwinian, devil–take–the–hindmost economy.

Honest failure is a common reality and may even have a salutary effect, though obviously not for those directly affected. The economist Schumpeter used the term "creative destruction" to describe a sort of cleansing effect as weaker and less efficient companies are swept out of existence.[2]

The U.S. legal system in particular appears to have shifted to where blame must be assigned and penalties levied in virtually every case of corporate failure, regardless of cause. The rest of the industrial world is deeply concerned about the spread to other jurisdictions of this litigious, expensive, and generally unhealthy practice. Director recruitment today is more difficult than even a decade ago. I hesitate to think about what it will be like in another ten years. Tort reform can help, but it must be serious and not merely playing around at the edges. At date of writing, this remains to be seen.

2. "Capitalism without bankruptcy is like Christianity without Hell" (Frank Borman)

Chapter 20

On the Frankness of Directors When Resigning from Boards

TO B(LAB) OR NOT TO B(LAB): that is the question … if irreverently put and with apologies to the Melancholy Dane.

In a column in the Report on Business section of the *Globe and Mail*, respected journalist Janet McFarland came out strongly in favour of directors speaking out openly and candidly when resigning from corporate boards.

Three quotes from that article convey the essence of her argument:

- "Shareholders appear to have no right to know why their elected representatives quit the boards of public companies, even when there may be serious issues that have driven them from their positions."

- "This sort of explanation[1] is far from adequate under the circumstances. Yet shareholders can do little about such vague disclosure, which has become standard in press releases."

- "At a conference last year, veteran director Matthew Gaasenbeek said the disclosure rule should be *compulsory*. It would give directors a clear forum for revealing concerns, he said. They would also have more protection from lawsuits. And the knowledge that such a report would have to be issued would give independent directors more clout in corporate disputes."

While these arguments supporting frank disclosure are appealing, I'm not convinced. I suppose the conspiracy of silence (or at least of platitudes) harks back to corporate governance's dark ages—twenty-five or more years ago—when directors really didn't matter that much and so what they said when they resigned was not very important. Or to resuscitate a contemptuous and much-quoted one-liner from that era, "Directors are like parsley on fish: decorative but useless." Ouch!

Today, when what directors do and say actually matter, voluntary resignation from a board is an event and what is said at the time by directors leaving is important. The explanations offered can influence shareholder views and investment decisions. So, at first blush, it seems reasonable that if directors are concerned enough about an issue to resign from a board, shareholders are entitled to understand those concerns, especially if they might have a depressing effect on share prices.

1. She noted that Brian Tobin, when resigning from two Magna boards and leaving a senior management position as well, had said publicly that he was "leaving to pursue other opportunities in the business world." A day earlier, Magna announced that Bill Davis had resigned from these same two boards "for personal and health reasons."

And yet there are some downsides to more transparent, candid disclosure, including the following:

SHARE PRICES

As I noted, share prices might be affected adversely. The counter-argument, of course, is that it's better for shareholders to learn of any serious problems sooner rather than later when they find their way eventually into the market. However, those who follow the ancient Roman advice—*praemonitus, premunitis* (forewarned is forearmed)—will prefer fair, true, clear—and early—disclosure over uncoordinated and sometimes biased comments by departing directors.

BOARDROOM CONFIDENTIALITY

Let's try another tack. Board collegiality is important and it can easily be shaken by adverse publicity caused by presenting only one side of what took place in the privacy of the boardroom. Too often, self-interest and bias would provoke unfair and even intemperate positions and public statements.

Although the analogy is not perfect, it's somewhat like cabinet solidarity and confidentiality. Washing in public the dirty linen of either a government or a corporation may be salutary quite a lot of the time but not always.

It depends on the issue and on its repercussions if disclosed, and especially if disclosed at the wrong time and prematurely by a director or small group of directors who in seeking to justify their actions may, as I said, present a partial or jaundiced view of an issue. They may also be angry, even vindictive. And that will not be helpful in the inevitable interviews that will be sought and sometimes granted after the release of a formal statement.

And then management and the remaining board members will inevitably be asked to respond publicly and will sometimes accede, if only in self-defence. A private disagreement might all too easily degenerate into a public squabble that could get out of hand and do more harm than good.

Consider an example. Assume that there is a deeply serious disagreement over some pivotal component of mission, vision, or strategy. Assume also that there are honest advocates on both sides of the issue. And assume finally that those on the losing side of the argument feel strongly enough to resign their directorships. What is served by deepening the wound by public disclosure and, inevitably, debate? What is accomplished by widening the debate to include those not close enough to the massive amount of context and detail to be able to contribute seriously to determining the best future direction for the enterprise?[2]

STRATEGIC CONSIDERATION

The media espouse openness reflexly, of course; it's in their bones.[3] But so do a company's competitors circling like sharks sensing blood and hoping to benefit from the asymmetrical fact that their own conflicts and weaknesses remain undisclosed if their own directors hang in there while another company's directors let it all hang out.

Furthermore, and to repeat for emphasis, if important and even crucial policy differences precipitate director resignations

2. Two quotes seem relevant here:
- "The opinion of 10,000 men is of no value if none of them knows anything about the subject." (Marcus Aurelius)
- "Truth is not determined by a majority vote." (Cardinal Ratzinger, now Pope Benedict XVI)

3. The U.S. First Amendment has been a powerful and far-reaching influence on journalists in democracies everywhere.

but help to clear the air and refocus a company, what is served by a public venting? There is insufficient upside to balance the downside of damaged reputations and weakened share prices.

OPEN DEBATE

Would frank and open debate at board level be muted or suppressed if every director was acutely aware that dissent serious enough to cause one or more resignations could trigger a public show–and–tell with unpleasant and potentially damaging consequences?

LEGAL LIABILITIES

Consider also the matter of directors' legal liabilities. If full disclosure were to be mandated by law, perhaps the resigning director would be sufficiently shielded. But then again, who could guarantee that, for example, a CEO who is criticized or even maligned publicly by one or more disgruntled directors wouldn't sue for libel or slander? Messy.

It need hardly be added that judgmental, disparaging public statements *not* protected by the law would be suicidal in today's chippy, litigious world. How likely is it that a law might be enacted to protect directors who speak out in public when they resign from a board? I defer to politicians and counsel except to say that it seems to me to be a mare's nest involving a labyrinth of subtle distinctions. I doubt that legislators and regulators would relish the task of trying to develop workable rules that would embrace the wide range of possible scenarios.

In theory, I might go so far as to support the view that some director resignations should be accompanied by explanations that go beyond the bland, anodyne, stereotypical reasons usually on offer. But other resignations, as discussed earlier, should not. In practice and to repeat, this means a judgment call on a case-by-case basis and opens a Pandora's box that Solomon and Sampson together would be unable to close.

VOLUNTARY RESIGNATIONS

It also seems to me that any voluntary resignation by one or more directors, even though accompanied as at present by only the most innocuous explanation(s), still sends a warning to experienced observers: journalists, analysts, business people in general. Must it always be spelled out publicly and blatantly in exquisite detail and damn the consequences? I concede that not all shareholders have acquired the mix of experience, sophistication, and intuitive "smarts" to draw the correct inferences. Some might take a company's disingenuously bland press release at face value. But, while caveat emptor in this scenario is not an acceptable rationale for non-disclosure, most shareholders who need advice seek it from those who are familiar with "spin" and know how to assess it.

NOT STANDING

Finally and importantly, what about directors who are asked, after careful consideration by a board chair and/or a governance and nominating committee, to resign or not stand for re-election? For whatever reason, they have been judged unsuitable or not up to the task. Must they endure the humiliation of admitting publicly that they've been sacked and why? If not, the fact that others must disclose, while they do not, implies the worst. Even those who really do resign for perfectly benign reasons, like health or overcommitment, would be suspect.

Chapter 21

Miscellaneous Musings

THIS CHAPTER DISCUSSES several quite different and, indeed, unrelated issues in contemporary governance: annual meetings; dual-class share structures and shareholder rights plans; setting director compensation: problems of process; and directors as agents or victims of change. Each raises important questions about directorship and corporate oversight in the present era of epidemic flimflammery, along with a dollop of crookery and book–cookery.

ANNUAL MEETINGS

The present protocol can be and often is badly misused. A recent *New York Times* article noted that the annual meeting of the Dana Corporation in the U.S. is held in the boardroom of the company's law firm, 430 miles from Dana's head office.

The meeting is chaired by a partner in that law firm. Neither the CEO nor any of the twelve other directors attend. In fact, Mr. Magliochetti, Dana's CEO, has not attended his company's annual meeting in fifteen years.

Another example. Both Morgan Stanley and Johnson Controls don't even invite their independent directors to their own annual meetings. And while the number of companies that follow this abhorrent practice is still small, it is growing.

Because Johnson Controls holds earlier conference calls to discuss earnings with analysts, it makes no presentation of any kind at its annual meetings. A few companies incorporated in states like Delaware have moved away from in-person annual meetings to virtual meetings that can only be attended electronically.

Some argue that these facades for genuine interaction among officers, directors, and shareholders are a defensive reaction to the Evelyn Davises[1] of the world. And certainly annual meetings have been disrupted and managements pilloried (sometimes unfairly).

There are, of course, illustrious exceptions to Dana's and others' mockery of shareholder democracy. The shining example is the legendary annual meeting of Berkshire Hathaway that includes a six-hour discussion, presided over by chairman Warren Buffet, that ranges across a wide spectrum of contemporary governance issues, including how investors can hold CEOs more accountable. And Berkshire Hathaway's own performance is dissected with as much transparency as any corporation anywhere. Has this detracted from performance?

1. Ms. Davis is well known in the U.S. for her flamboyant presence and comments at corporate annual meetings.

Hardly. Over several decades, it has been more than exemplary; it has been spectacular.

But in turning away from the worst and the best to the typical, I ask myself whether the time-worn annual meeting ritual needs a major overhaul. Is there a better way? To start with, the formal part of the process is so highly stylized that it's largely kabuki theatre, only duller. Directors are elected and external auditors are appointed with all the grave formality that accompanies a *fait accompli*. Special resolutions, except rarely, have already been decided by proxies solicited earlier. It has parallels to the coronation of a hereditary monarch: confirmation of the inevitable.

The customary role of directors at AGMs is, when introduced as having been elected for another year, to rise from a front-row seat, turn around, smile engagingly, and sit down again. As Woody Allen once said about life in general, "Ninety percent of the time, all you have to do is show up."

An annual show-and-tell may have been informative enough and frequent enough when the business world moved more slowly, when technology was more primitive, when merger and acquisition activity was more muted, when widely held companies weren't thrust more often, though unwillingly, into an auction, and when most investors sought long-term value.

Today's investment horizon is shorter; too often, it is too short. Speculators are as common as investors. Even the once-infamous day trader has re-emerged, if shyly and tentatively, apparently unabashed by the bloodbath of a few years ago but still with an attention span of fifteen minutes.

To repeat, is there a better way? Here are a few ideas, some more practical than others, that have been put forward on how to improve communication between an enterprise and its shareholder-owners:

- Annual-meeting proxies should include voting for or against (not merely "withhold") individual directors along with accompanying concise resumés as well as information on board and committee attendance.

- A more aggressive step is to allow investors holding, collectively, some designated percentage of issued shares to collaborate on the nomination of up to, say, two independent directors. The details of how this would work in practice need to be thought through in-depth but the principle is, I think, sound. By that I mean that the risk of greater difficulty in maintaining board collegiality may well be justified by a stronger influence of ownership on governance practices as well as by a greater likelihood of fresh thinking.

- A still more controversial proposal requires shareholders to vote for and elect one fewer director than the number of names on the slate. Call it Darwinian musical chairs. The presumed advantage of holding a real election with winners and losers would, in my view, be more than offset by the greater difficulty in attracting quality directors, a chronic problem with elections in the political arena. On the whole, I don't think this idea has much merit.

- Directors should play more proactive, less perfunctory, roles at annual meetings. The chairs of key board committees—audit, compensation and human resources, governance and nominating, and perhaps others, depending on the industry and company—should present personal views on the work of their respective committees over the year under review. Such reports should be much more than carefully edited, risk-free, dry-as-dust recitations of the obvious, drafted by a lawyer and carefully screened by both senior management and a PR practitioner.

- The annual-meeting format should be supplemented by proactive quarterly meetings. These should combine an in-person meeting at one site with a well-designed webcast for investors who can't be there live. At both the annual and such quarterly meetings, consider skipping the canapés, the lunch, the music, the fanfare, even some of the great graphics. This will leave more time to concentrate on full and candid communication, as well as on an attentive response to questions, comments, and suggestions from investors.

- At all public meetings, avoid a canned recitation of what was in the annual or quarterly report and what any conscientious shareholder has already read and digested. Strive for freshness and for a fair balance between opportunities and risks. While securities regulators are taking an increasingly hard line on overpromising, many CEOs are still more tempted to exaggerate the opportunities and downplay the risks than the reverse.

In summary, most of these concessions to greater shareholder democracy and to investor confidence may not be earth-shaking, but they are small steps in the right direction.

DUAL-CLASS SHARE STRUCTURES

Two very different perspectives on dual-class share structures are captured under the next two bullets.

- Consider the situation where a founder and controlling shareholder owns a class of shares with anywhere from as low as two to as high as a thousand votes per share. A minority shareholder, who bought shares later when the founder took the company public, owns shares in a different class with one vote per share. The *status quo*, whether financial results are good, bad, or indifferent, is typically perpetuated with little or no recourse.

  This is so clearly inimical to legitimate minority shareholder rights that many such shareholders, along with many financial advisors, business writers, and pundits who opine on this sort of thing, are outraged. They conclude that any remedy short of outlawing dual–class share structures—perhaps staged over, say, five years—is insufficient.

- On the other hand, a 2005 analysis by Derek DeCloet, investor analyst for the *Globe and Mail*, as reported by *Toronto Star* business columnist David Olive in *The Corporate Ethics Monitor* leads one to a different conclusion. It noted that dual–class share companies in the S and P/TSX composite index and that had been publicly traded for at least ten years produced an average annual return of 16.1 percent. The same statistic for all companies in the index was 10 percent. And that included, of course, the higher–yielding dual-class share companies.

  Companies in the dual–class share category included such stellar performers as Alimentation Couche-Tard Inc., Four

Seasons Hotels, George Weston Ltd., Jean Coutu Group, and Transcontinental Inc.

Several notorious examples were given of single–class share companies that Mr. Olive described as "models of strategic ineptitude." I decline to name them, not to protect the guilty but to help protect the innocent (me) from some sort of chippy lawsuit.

How do we reconcile such disparate views? Not easily. And what reasonable prescription can be put forward? While finessing the vexing issue of whether dual-class shares are, on average, a boon or a boondoggle, I'd like to examine the related question of what might take their place if they were legislated out of existence. I submit that something would be needed, although not to perpetuate a founder in power when his shareholdings may be as low as one or two percent of the issued equity. But there is still a need to consider the interests of all shareholders of an enterprise that, in order to facilitate rapid growth, has gone public and given away voting control. This exposes the company to a hostile takeover bid that may or may not be in the best interests of the company, its employees and its shareholders. Such a bid could be premature: too early in the company's evolution. Or it could simply be a lowball offer with no one else bidding to raise the ante.

As a minimum, given a hostile bid, more time is usually needed than is available to solicit a higher bid from those white knights who usually don't appear at the castle door on demand. More time can be gained in two different ways:

- Regulatory requirements as to how long a bid must remain open, in order to encourage and facilitate a higher competitive bid, can be lengthened. In the heat of battle, the process of finding another bidder frequently requires more time than the law now mandates.

- A "vanilla" shareholder rights plan can be put in place. I recognize that it's an exercise in careful legal drafting to buy time without also entrenching management. But it can be done and it comes down, of course, as much to intent as to language. Here a strong board is essential to strike the best balance between gaining more time to access carefully the alternatives and making conditions too difficult for any buyers, friendly or otherwise, to come to the table.

But, while buying more time to respond to a hostile takeover bid is highly desirable in order to allow genuine market values to surface, this fails to deal with another dark cloud that hangs over too many companies, especially in the earlier years. What protects the founder who gave up voting control to facilitate rapid growth but is absolutely convinced that he or she can guide the enterprise to further undreamt-of heights and to share prices that dwarf those of today?

Some will say that the founder accepted that risk when he or she went public. *Caveat venditor*: let the seller beware. On the other hand, several U.S. states—Delaware, for example—protect directors who reject a hostile takeover bid, even at a share price substantially above current market, if they can convince the court that they did so for the right reasons. That is, their real and not merely their stated rationale must be to maximize shareholder value, not to entrench management ... and themselves. But in other jurisdictions, once a company is in play, it is almost inevitable that a takeover of some kind will follow and another corporation will bite the dust.[2] That will sometimes but not always be in the best interests of the selling shareholders.

Where directors are free to reject a bid for the right reasons, it is, of course, crucial that the interests of all shareholders be considered and not merely those of the founders who have given up equity control but continue to hold enough power, often via dual-share structures, that they may prefer a second-best but certain price today to a higher (even after discounted for the time-value of money) but uncertain price tomorrow. That is, some proportion of all founders—especially those who have been at it for a long time—may opt for certainty over future risk and strife and perhaps for the allure of the standard of living and more relaxed lifestyle that a high and secure net worth can provide.

On the other hand, some founders may have either an unrealistic and inflated view of what they have created or no interest whatsoever in selling and retiring, regardless of how high a price is offered. Either situation may not be in the best interests of minority shareholders. Reconciling these kinds of sensitive trade-offs requires a board with both judgment/wisdom and intestinal fortitude. A board's ability to influence these decisions will, of course, vary greatly with the founder's percentage of the voting share outstanding.

2. Unfortunate, but that's the way our system works. Or is it something more? Entrepreneurs and founders, collectively, are an important, indeed crucial, part of our economy and society. In the May 2005 issue of *ca magazine*, Gérard Bérubé of Montréal's *Le Devoir* noted that 70 percent of businesses in Canada are family-owned, that they represent more than 50 percent of GDP and half of all salaries paid, and that they create two-thirds of new jobs.

SETTING DIRECTOR COMPENSATION: PROBLEMS OF PROCESS

The determinants of compensation for board service are comparatively simple in substance but more difficult and sensitive in form.

The simple part refers to the fact that there are lots of good and current surveys out there that provide the necessary hard data, broken out by industry and by company size, while also identifying the key choices and variables in common use. These include annual retainer levels for both the chairman and directors, the use or not (and size of) a per–meeting fee, use or not of retainers for board committee chairs and members, payment or not for travel time, other paid expenses, and use of any perquisites.

The much more sensitive issue is who should approve any changes in director compensation. Incidentally, a decade or two ago, fees were looked at and revised only about once every three or four years. But in today's world of rapidly escalating workloads and risks for directors, fees are and should be at least evaluated, if not acted upon, annually.

There are two groups or individuals that can and do, but definitely should not, approve changes to director compensation. The first of these is the CEO or any part of management, including the head of human resources or some management committee. The board approves CEO and other executive management compensation and, if the CEO or part of his organization determines director compensation, the result is a blatantly unacceptable example of two groups washing each other's laundry.

The same argument can be used, *a fortiori*, against the board chair or a committee of the board or the board as a whole setting director compensation, with or without the support of an external consultant. While I have no doubt that the great majority of boards would handle such an assignment responsibly and might even lean to below-average compensation on the grounds that Caesar's wife must be beyond reproach, the optics are unacceptably bad. And these days, optics matter. Attention must be paid.

And yet other of the above two processes or some variant of them is used today by the great majority of companies in the U.S. and Canada. It seems to me that a better approach involves these steps:

- A fully independent consultant with no other assignments of any kind from a company is hired to do the necessary research and to make recommendations to the chairman or a board committee. And while I recognize that even a single-assignment consultant still knows who pays his bills, such an assignment will very rarely be large enough to influence the judgment of a reputable consulting firm.

- The consultant's recommendations are reviewed carefully by a committee of the board, usually the human resources and compensation committee, and then by the full board.

- The resulting carefully considered recommendations are then included in the materials sent to all shareholders in advance of the next annual general meeting.

- Proxies are, of course, sought on this and any other matters up for shareholder approval. At the AGM, a formal vote is taken and recorded. On director compensation, a simple majority in favour of the recommendations is enough for approval and implementation.

This approach is a little more complicated but ethically and optically beyond reproach. It comes as close to best practice as an inherently sensitive job permits.

A potential concern with this least worst of the choices available is that shareholders, collectively, will fail to understand and be sympathetic to the problems of directors in the brave new world of governance with much larger commitments of their time and much more serious risks to their reputations and pocketbooks. Although the dollars involved are usually insignificant in relation to a company's size, some shareholder groups may take a simplistic zero–sum position: if there's more for you, there's less for me. Or they may choose to punish the directors for any performance deficiencies, serious or otherwise. Ultimately, it's up to the board chair and the external consultant to make the case for upward adjustment as cogently as the situation allows. After that, it's so be it.

As I noted earlier, this recommended approach is certainly not yet the norm. But I believe it should be and I predict it will be and not many years from now at that.

DIRECTORS: AGENTS OR VICTIMS OF CHANGE?

A recent public outcry about the role of a board in a high-profile scandal involved accounting irregularities and misstatement of earnings at Nortel Networks. And for those who follow these things, it's a repeat of earlier, eerily similar examples of

Nortel's financial mismanagement. And the subsequent share price decline demonstrated the truth of that old saying: "Fool me once, shame on you; fool me twice, shame on me."

The Nortel board of 2004 was composed of many distinguished individuals but, at least from the outside, they appeared to be pawns more than potentates.[3] As with other boards embroiled in messes of one kind or another, they left the impression of being more at the mercy of events than in charge and providing the strong, in-control oversight so badly needed. The problem lay with the board collectively, not with the directors as individuals.[4]

Today, perhaps more than ever before, the free enterprise system is viewed with suspicion, even enmity. It's at least as bad as in the trust-busting days of a century ago and the scandals of later booms like the twenties, the eighties and the nineties.

Have directors as a class failed in their obligations to society? And is this why other players have moved into the breach and are now playing stronger, tougher, more central roles? This includes lawmakers and regulators, the media, including the business press, and investors, both individual and institutional. These latter in particular have flexed their muscles, civilly so far, by and large, but unmistakably. An excellent example is the relatively new Canadian Coalition for Good Governance. Had Canadian directors as a class been fulfilling their obligations more vigorously, perhaps there might have been less need for such a body to be created.

3. *Pawns or Potentates?* is the name of an excellent governance book of several years ago by Professor Jay Lorsch of HBS.
4. In the *New York Times* of May 13, 2004, I was quoted (accurately) as saying, "It's a very distinguished board. Who would they recruit who's any better than what they've got?"

I believe that North America first and foremost, but the industrial democracies in general, if somewhat later, are moving slowly but inexorably to a different balance of power between management and shareholders. Power is shifting to constituencies who are prepared to act on the conviction that business must serve shareholders (and certain other stakeholders in defined circumstances), not management. Boards could have led this charge but have largely failed to do so. If we cut through all the verbiage and obfuscation, CEOs[5] are employees like everyone else in a corporation, albeit usually extraordinarily well-paid ones.

And founders? Their real and richly deserved rewards should come from the increased value of their shareholdings. And who can argue with that? The shareholder class in general, both individual and institutional, can hardly disagree. But founders in their management roles should be paid like everyone else at levels that a truly functioning competitive market would dictate and that effective boards and compensation committees could support in all good conscience and without crossed fingers behind backs.

But back to the issue of whether or not directors are agents or victims of change. It is not, I think, too harsh a judgment to conclude that directors have delegated power far too often to managements that have abused that power too often.

To be fair, the game has been rigged against independent directors for reasons discussed elsewhere in this book. But

5. This includes even those celebrity CEOs that make the covers of national magazines, though not as frequently now as in the nineties, that decade of glory for those captains of capitalism who enjoyed the adulation of millions via mass-circulation media.

whether the game is fair or not, rigged or not, independent directors as a class have a long and difficult road to climb to strengthen their authority as central and primary intermediaries between managements and shareholders. It is important that they do so.

Corporate and Not-for-Profit Governance: Similarities and Differences[1]

IT SEEMS APPROPRIATE here to discuss governance in three parts:

- What distinguishes governance in the not-for-profit sector (using universities as a proxy for not-for-profit institutions in general) from that in the corporate sector?
- What are the crucial ingredients of first-class governance that transcend sectors?
- How good is governance today in each sector?

1. This article is an edited and updated version of a speech given in Halifax in 2003 to the Canadian Association of University Business Officers.

Let's begin with intersectoral differences. Perhaps the most profound as well as obvious difference lies in what constituency the enterprise seeks to serve.

In the corporate sector, mainstream thinking, supported by most legal theory and laws, is that the principal goal is to serve the corporation which then translates into the shareholder. Other stakeholders—customers, suppliers, employees, government, the environment, society and the public good—act as constraints on shareholder interests.

The legitimacy of those constraints varies enormously from issue to issue, from country to country, and from corporation to corporation. Conservative economists espouse the view—discredited widely in some societies and partly discredited in all—that the only legitimate goal is shareholder maximization. Milton Friedman, the nonagenarian champion and early proponent of this position, has argued, for example, that corporations should not make donations to charitable causes, no matter how deserving, on the grounds that profits belong only to shareholders who can, if they choose, donate to deserving charities themselves.

However, over the past couple of decades, there has emerged a more progressive view—the stakeholder model—in which each relevant constituency has some sort of legitimate claim on the corporate purse. And that claim is as strong within its sphere of influence as that of the shareholder within its sphere of influence.

I should add that, while the stakeholder model has gained many adherents and some acceptance in Western Europe, this is not yet the case in North America where it has received, for the most part, some support in theory but little more than lip service in practice. When push comes to shove, only a very few brave, unusually secure, and/or idealistic CEOs would routinely value the claimed rights of any stakeholder as highly as those of shareholders except in a few very specific and clearly defined areas.

It is clear, I am sure, that adherence to the shareholder model simplifies the role of directors. A single-minded focus on the bottom line concentrates the mind wonderfully, as Dr. Johnson once said about a man facing the prospect of being hung.

By contrast, in the not-for-profit sector, there is no predominant constituency or stakeholder, although I do not doubt that, in any given institution, several constituencies are each convinced that their own roles and needs are paramount or at least should be.

In the university system, not only are there several important stakeholders but Solomon himself could not assign any enduring hierarchy or priority. Depending on the issue, any one of several constituencies can claim primacy. My intent here is not to attempt vainly to sort out precedence but simply to note that the role of a university governor and indeed the role of academic leadership and administration is complicated and, at times, compromised by these groups competing for advantage measured, as often as not, in terms of available funding.

A second and perhaps related difference between corporate and university governance is that corporations are more hierarchical. Systems of chain of command, especially in larger, well-established corporations, are more rigid and closer to, indeed founded on, the military model.

Universities certainly recognize the need for structure, but hierarchy is not held in high esteem in all nooks and crannies of the academic world. And so the organization chart is flatter and there is much more contact, both formal and informal, that bypasses and ignores formal structure.

This does not, however, mean that process is less important in universities than in corporations. Quite the contrary. Perhaps because hierarchy is not widely held in high regard at universities, a set of rather detailed policies and procedures often takes its place, partly as a kind of defensive reaction to a more casual approach to structure and reporting.

And how does this affect governance in the two sectors? To which the answer, or so it appears to me, is "not much." However, a governor or trustee or council member in the university sector needs to keep in mind always that universities and corporations are very different in their collective attitudes towards hierarchy and precedence.

As a single example, most faculty members I've known and worked with over the years believe that what they're accomplishing in research and teaching is at least as important as what happens in university administration. And because first-class research and teaching are at the heart of what a university is all about, it's not altogether surprising that this attitude exists.

Of course, in reality, a properly functioning university (or hospital or school board) is like a symphony orchestra in which little worthwhile is accomplished unless all of the instruments play/work together in close harmony.

Nevertheless, a robust individualism is found more frequently, though certainly not exclusively, in universities than in corporations and that's not such a bad thing, although it's best in moderation. Too much veers towards anarchy.

A third area of compare and contrast is the kinds of directors and governors sought after and appointed in corporations and universities.

In both sectors, there is still a lingering propensity to recruit "names" for no especially sound reason other than that they look good in appointment notices and annual reports. And a generous sprinkling of "names" might even help to recruit other board members.

Sometimes "names" make a serious contribution to an organization and sometimes they don't. I hope that I am not being naïvely optimistic when I say that most boards today, in contrast to those of, say, twenty years ago, are less bedazzled by celebrities and especially by those who aren't prepared to pull their weight.

In the corporate world, particularly in the sobering post-Enron world, directors are sought more than in earlier times for their strength of character, their independence, their experience, their judgment and even, rare as this quality is, for their wisdom.

I can attest that this was not the norm a generation ago when new directors were chosen mostly because they were friends or colleagues of those already in the well-known old boys' club. Typically, the board met once a quarter from ten until noon after which a long and convivial lunch was convened, often accompanied by vintages with which even the most dedicated oenophile could find no fault. That day is long gone and good riddance.

In some parts of the not-for-profit sector, the old "give, get, or get off" philosophy is still alive and well. This is especially true with boards in the cultural arena—ballet, opera, symphony—where ticket sales are rarely enough to cover full costs and so philanthropic support is crucial.

Where government pays most[2] of the costs (hospitals) or at least some of them (universities) through tuition, research grants, and capital support, the "give, get, or get off" philosophy is, if not absent, at least subdued. And as user-pay becomes even more significant, this rather narrow, even cynical approach to director selection will become still less common.

Universities have been moving up the user-pay scale for some time, as government funding has failed to keep pace even with inflation. And only legitimate and important concerns about accessibility and fairness have slowed the broader and more aggressive movement to higher user-pay that some professional faculties in some universities have already embraced.

So while the fund-raising or fund-giving abilities of university board members are not, nor should they be, ignored, other characteristics are generally given more weight. It seems to me that universities today are seeking the same qualities in their board members as the best corporations. They are recruited for the quality of their advice and because they will supplement and complement the experience and make-up of university administrators and work faithfully and diligently towards common goals.

In that best of all possible worlds, two usually quite different sets of experiences combine in university governance to bring about that overused word "synergy," that is, a felicitous

2. In Canada, though not in the U.S.

fit between disparate sets of backgrounds and skills in administrations and in boards.

Let me comment briefly on the size of boards. In the corporate world, boards have been shrinking. A recent study by Patrick O'Callaghan noted that roughly half of Canada's 300 largest corporations now have boards of between six and nine members with the very largest at twenty-two. A generation ago, the Canadian Imperial Bank of Commerce had fifty-five members.

With boards bigger than perhaps fifteen members, speechmaking tends to replace serious discussion. And the locus of decision shifts from the full board to an executive committee, along with a generous assortment of functional committees.

As corporate boards have grown smaller, executive committees have become less common. In the corporate world, they are, in fact, an endangered species. Global telephony has facilitated this evolution. And an important side benefit of their approaching demise is that directors are no longer classified into two categories: those on the inside and in the know and everyone else.

In the university sector, boards are much larger for various reasons but certainly because more constituencies need to be represented. The York University board, during my time as chair, had thirty-six members, plus or minus. And while I haven't seen any recent statistics, I believe that the all-university mean is about the same. As noted, large boards make executive committees essential and so most university governance systems have one.

I'd like now to comment briefly on the issue of diversity in board composition. Corporate boards continue to be highly homogeneous in terms of the functional backgrounds of their members. The great majority are either active or retired senior corporate executives, most commonly board chairs or presidents. This mix is leavened by the addition of a sprinkling of retired politicians, men and women with a professional background in law, accounting, consulting, or medicine, and academics, usually either university presidents or deans of professional faculties.

University boards are much more diverse by background of member, reflecting the greater diversity of constituencies that should be represented. This richer mix is, on balance, a good thing. While it takes a first-class chair and some forbearance to ensure that greater diversity doesn't lead to greater disharmony, the upside is a wider range of views expressed on any given issue. With skilful leadership and integration, this ought to result in better decisions. And often it does.

Then there's diversification by race and gender. Most corporate boards today have at least one woman director. But only 5 percent of the 300 largest Canadian public companies have two and a mere handful have three or more. The U.S. record is somewhat better but still not good enough. With respect to visible minorities, the record, to be blunt about it, is abysmal. There has been some talk, but almost no movement.

With universities, the record, measured by either gender or race, is better by a wide margin. This reflects, among other things, both student and staff diversity and, to a lesser but steadily increasing degree, faculty diversity. And who can argue with the proposition that a university's board should be representative of its constituents and that a university's faculty and staff and student body should be representative of the communities they serve? Those who espouse stakeholder capitalism likely feel that this should apply equally to corporations. Those who believe in or at least practice shareholder capitalism likely disagree.

I cannot move on without a passing reference to one obvious difference between corporate directors and those in the not-for-profit sector. Corporations pay their directors; not-for-profits don't. In Canada today, the mean annual compensation, all-in, of a director of one of the some 250 companies in the TSX composite index is about $60,000. Furthermore, as one result of a relentless increase in corporate director responsibilities and the time required to fulfill them, compensation is likely to continue to increase over the next few years. Not-for-profit board members receive no stipend, unless psychic income counts. In fact, subject to ability to pay, governors, trustees, and directors are expected to contribute generously to capital and other campaigns of increasing frequency and duration.

Are paid corporate directors more likely than unpaid volunteer board members to be seriously committed to the vision, mission, and goals of an enterprise, to make a larger contribution to its success, to believe more fervently in what they're doing, or to work any harder? The clear answer is not at all. Despite cynical opinion to the contrary, I have observed over the years that the heart is at least as strong a motivator as the pocketbook.

Turn with me now to the second question raised at the beginning of this chapter. If first-class governance transcends sectors, as I believe that it largely does, what are its common and crucial ingredients? Let me name five.

First is the happy combination of a strong effective chair and a strong, effective president: two competent individuals who can work together in harmony. This makes the obvious assumption that we are talking about two different people. In the not-for-profit sector, this is taken for granted. In the corporate sector, it is not, at least not quite yet.

My second point is to re-emphasize how crucial it is that a strong chair and a strong CEO each recognize that a board and an administration must work closely together. In terms of logic and common sense, this is unassailable. But the potential downside of two strong persons working in tandem is a turf battle that turns the asset of strength through union into the liability of dysfunction. To avoid this, both chair and CEO must learn how to work together in collaborative harmony. Easy to say. Harder to do. It means recognition by each that the other has a legitimate and important role to play. Each must respect both the role of the other and the other person as an individual.

There must also be a mutual recognition that, in our imperfect and untidy world, roles and boundaries will not always be crystal clear. And so the two individuals and the two organizations that stand behind those two individuals must work maturely and respectfully to clarify ambiguities. This process is unending. There will always be issues in which both parties have a stake and so power must be shared responsibly. While this is a most hazardous sea to navigate successfully, it can be done and, in the best organizations, it is being done.

My third crucial ingredient involves the “tone” of the enterprise, a quality which is influenced by its history, traditions, and blend of triumphs and disappointments but most strongly by its current leadership. Finding and maintaining the right tone is a demanding test of that leadership.

An effective board is neither a love-in nor a bear pit. We have all seen “cheerleader” boards in which everyone spends too much time congratulating everyone else on accomplishments, however slight, real or imagined, while ignoring the important strategic questions that determine the future of the enterprise. As I once wrote elsewhere, a board must not be, to quote the old song, like "home, home on the range ... where never is heard a discouraging word." Obviously this fosters complacency and an aversion to tackling the tough issues.

On the other hand, it is equally important that a board not be chronically negative. Petty faultfinding, cynical, embittered or angry rants, *ad hominem* attacks, are all hallmarks of a destructive tone which invariably means serious trouble. The best boards feel free to discuss weaknesses but with the constructive intent to do something to correct them. At the same time, strengths and accomplishments are recognized but neither disproportionately nor in a self-congratulatory way. Balance, balance, balance.

The fourth crucial component of effective governance in any organization is so obvious that I mention it only because too many boards in both sectors devote too little time to it. That is, the best boards regularly visit and revisit vision, mission, strategy, and multi-year goals.

This is not, of course, something that is on the agenda of every meeting although every decision of any consequence must be taken in the context of these overarching considerations. Thinking strategically must become ingrained or "embedded," to use the currently fashionable term. That is, a good executive and a good director or governor must avoid the mindset of the Parisian cat burglar who considered himself a thief only when he was actually stealing.

At any given time, the vision, mission, strategy, and goals of an enterprise must be as clear in the minds of every board member as regular, focused discussion can make them. Annual board retreats of a day or two are one good way to help accomplish this.

Finally, a good board in either sector does not micromanage. However, having said that, it is equally important that a board be informed routinely—that is, regularly and fully—on matters that lie principally and even totally within management's purview. This does not mean formal approval for approval's sake. Empty approval without enough knowledge to disapprove is a form of institutional hypocrisy. And it flies in the face of my earlier comment about having as clear a division of responsibilities between board and management as a complex world permits.

The rationale for wanting to keep boards informed on matters where responsibility rests squarely with management is that a board that focuses solely on broad principles and strategic issues can too easily become isolated from the culture—from the day-to-day hustle and bustle, from the flow of information about people and events—that shape the context in which larger, more strategic decisions are made.

I have seen this happen in both sectors and the unhappy result is a disconnect between board policy-setting and management execution. The price of bridging this divide is more trees converted to paper and more glasses for weary eyes, but the price of not doing it is greater still. To repeat, for full and frank information flow to add value and not subtract it, both board and management must be vigilant to ensure that there is universal respect for that important, if sometimes amorphous and shifting, boundary between what each body is responsible for.

The third and final question that I'd like to address briefly can, for the most part, be answered only subjectively. How good is governance today in corporations and in universities, and is it better and perhaps even different than, say, twenty years ago?

Let me begin with corporate governance where recent improvement has been considerable, though much remains to be done. Most of this progress has been in response to serious problems and external pressures for change. There has been much talk about a crisis of confidence. Certainly the number of recent failures and the magnitude of fraudulent behaviour have provoked some strong, even evangelical, responses. And since failure of governance has been widely viewed as part of the problem, comprehensive changes in governance have been proposed and many have already been implemented.

Pressured by law-makers and regulators, goaded by investors, fearful of lawsuits, shamed by negative publicity and public outrage, corporations and their governance have moved into an era where boards have more power in relation to managements and where regulatory bodies have more power in relation to corporations. It remains to be seen whether the culture will shift permanently or whether recidivism and reversion to old norms will prevail.

In Canada, the decline in confidence has been somewhat less dramatic, perhaps because most of the more recent high-profile corporate fiasco have been U.S.–based. Though who knows whether and when we'll have a shameful new example of our own to match such earlier cases as Bre-X, Confederation

Life, Dylex, Livent, and YBM Magnex, along with more current ones, like Royal Group Technologies, and the hierarchy of companies in the troubled world of Lord Black?

To be fair about it, the quality of corporate governance in Canada has been slowly improving over the years, especially in the past decade. And there is little doubt that, more recently, this has accelerated dramatically as Canadian corporations look nervously over their shoulders at what's been going on south of the border. In this regard, I am reminded of the relevance of that old English proverb: "It's an ill wind that blows no one any good." That is, problems can lead to solutions.

And so Canadian directors today, compared to those of a generation ago, are more conscientious, harder-working, better educated and trained, more aware of their need to play a stronger, more proactive role in the effective governance of corporations.

Am I describing a panacea, a veritable Renaissance of corporate behaviour and governance? Hardly. Using only my own experience and subjective judgment, I would say that, on a scale of one to ten, the quality of corporate governance in Canada has improved over the past two decades from perhaps 2½ to 7, a very considerable and much needed change. However, more needs to be done and backsliding is always a risk.

And what of the university sector? It seems to me that the quality of governance has steadily improved over the years. It's true that there has been no galvanizing impact arising out of the crisis of confidence in the corporate sector where too much executive power has led to blatant abuses and excesses of the worst kind. But there has been another kind of crisis, a more gradual, evolving problem reminiscent of that story, apocryphal or not, about lobsters not screaming if the temperature in the pot is raised slowly enough. I refer, of course, to inadequate government funding of higher education. And while the severity of the problem varies with the jurisdiction, the level of funding in general has failed for years to keep pace even with inflation, which is itself not much of a standard against which to be measured.

Faced with a problem of this gravity, university administrations and boards recognize that they need each other more than ever on the classic assumption that "if we don't hang together, we'll all hang separately." There is a common recognition that close collaboration in a common cause against short-sighted policy is advanced by sound governance.

It is true, as I said much earlier, that the multi-constituency nature of a modern university with several objectives, often in conflict with another and not always easily measured, makes the job of both board and administration more complex and difficult than in the corporate sector. Balancing the interests of one constituency against another, valuing one objective against another, is a little like playing three-dimensional chess, much more complex than regular chess.

Despite these hurdles, not insurmountable but formidable, my impression is that university boards are rising to their contemporary challenges. Perhaps the consciousness of boards in both sectors has been raised by the long litany of recent corporate failures in which both managements and boards have been implicated. All boards understand today more clearly than ever before that while they should not, must not, and indeed cannot, *manage*, in any real sense of the word, they must be more diligent, more aggressive, more persistent overseers of those who do manage.

In a democracy, everyone must be accountable either to another individual or body of individuals. This means genuine, at times sharp-edged, accountability in which, regardless of challenges and complexities, high performance is demanded and achieved. In a dictatorship, this accountability principle is renounced with predictable consequences. This was illustrated zanily but memorably in an off-the-wall film of a decade or more ago called *A History of the World, Part I.* In it, Mel Brooks, as a despotic ruler, uttered that unforgettable line, "It's good to be a king!" And surely, for absolute monarchs and dictators, it is, but not for their subjects.

Imperial CEOs and intellectually arrogant university presidents may once have enjoyed a certain vogue but, in a democratic society, teamwork at all levels and in every sector, including close ties between management and boards, is more likely to produce superior results over the long run.

Chapter 23
A Personal Take on Ethics

LET'S STEP BACK from the day-to-day and talk more philosophically about why ethical behaviour should matter to each of us as individuals and about abuses caused by its absence. On a personal level, I need to go back to 1987 to answer in any coherent way the question "What does ethical behaviour mean and why does it matter?"

That year, I had been invited by a friend, Claude Taylor, then CEO of Air Canada, to speak about business ethics at the opening plenary session of the Governor General's Study Conference in Calgary. The audience comprised some 200 bright young men and women in their twenties and thirties from all walks of life who had been brought together for several intensive weeks of interaction and learning. In preparing for that speech, I reflected at length on what ethics was all about.

And I became convinced that this was a subject that mattered both to society and to me.

During most of the eighties and before the recession of the early nineties, there were so many examples of dishonesty, corruption, and greed run amok that, in the U.S., though certainly not limited to that country, it became a national scandal. Many will remember the flood of best-selling books with titles like *Bonfire of the Vanities*, *Liar's Poker*, *Predator's Ball*, and *Barbarians at the Gate*.

In 1985, Ivan Boesky ended a speech at Harvard Business School by raising his arms above his head in a "V for victory" pose and saying, "So here's to greed!" He was wildly applauded. This was parodied a year or so later in the movie *Wall Street* when the mythical mogul Gordon Gekko solemnly pronounced that "Greed is good." Another example of art imitating life.

In 1989, Michael Milken pleaded guilty to six counts of felony and was sentenced to ten years in jail; he served three. He also paid a record US$600 million in fines and restitution, having earned almost that amount in 1988 alone. At the time of his incarceration, his known net worth was a couple of billion dollars. In fairness, he has devoted much of his post-imprisonment time to various good works.

From 1987 to 1993, I gave two dozen speeches on some or other aspect of business ethics to just about any organization that would listen. But then one day I stopped, largely because I'd said what I wanted to say and was starting to repeat myself. Furthermore, it was getting harder not to sound sanctimonious, pious, and/or evangelical. The last thing I wanted was to sound like some demented religious fanatic.

Let me try to sum up briefly my beliefs on this topic, although nothing is simple any more.

First, merely staying on the right side of the law is not enough. Although, for some, even that is too much to ask. The law is, of course, of overarching importance. Without it, chaos rules. But the law as a regulator of ethical behaviour is usually too little and invariably too late. The law sets boundaries that separate those on the right side from those on the wrong side who, if caught and convicted, pay fines and/or go to jail. But it's instructive to remember that those who play the game close to the boundaries, who flirt with the law, are only a hair's breadth away from being a felon. Not good enough.

Now let me make it clear that there's nothing wrong with wanting to enjoy the good life made possible by earning enough money to sustain it. However, some of the sordid excesses of, first, the eighties, then the nineties, and still today, pose dangers to the long-term stability of our economic system.

Let me give you a few examples:

- In 1960, the CEO of an S&P 500 company in the U.S. earned 20 times what the average U.S. factory worker earned. By 1988, this had grown to 40 times. By 2001, it had mushroomed to a spectacular 450 times. And for the largest 100 S&P companies, it had soared to an astonishing 1000 times.

- Until Ross Johnson, a Canadian by birth, lost control of RJR Nabisco in 1990, he enjoyed a corporate lifestyle that beggared those of emperors and kings. The company's airplane hangar contained ten jets, twenty-six pilots, and an adjoining three-story building replete with such sumptuous décor as Italian-marble floors, inlaid-mahogany walls, extensive Japanese gardens, and Old Masters. Who paid? The shareholders. Who else? And yet his excesses were not unusual except perhaps in sheer brazenness.

- Today we have senior executives who negotiate contracts that, in the event of a hostile takeover of their company, pay out as much as hundreds of millions of dollars, even if the new owners beseech them to stay on. The purpose of such clauses—in addition to feeding greed—is to dissuade anyone from making a control bid in the first place. Should such a bid be made anyway, management of the target company is rewarded in princely fashion. The *Wall Street Journal* once referred, rather indelicately, to this practice as the golden condom because it protects senior management while screwing the shareholder.

- It's been reported that Carly Fiorina, formerly of Hewlett-Packard, and Michael Capellas, formerly of Compaq, received an additional US$117 million between them for merging their two companies. This raises a simple question. What on earth are CEOs already being extraordinarily well paid for?

- Some option grants to CEOs and other senior executives have been obscenely large. For example, Michael Eisner made the news a few years ago when he received US$500 of Disney options.

The worst part of option grants is that, far too often, they have been exercised with quite unbelievable payouts to the recipients while the companies themselves have later either flamed out, like Enron and many others, or lost most of their value, like Nortel and many others. As the former head of Quaker Oats, Ken Mason, once said, "The beauty of most compensation schemes is that they always reward performance ... no matter how dismal it is."

I've never met a saint, though I don't doubt that they exist. I'm sure that most of them would be hard to live with. And there are few people who could live up to the ideals of the late U.S. senator Claude Pepper who, when asked, near the end of his long life, what he'd like inscribed on his tombstone, replied: "He loved God and his fellow man and tried to serve both."

Still, I believe and I think most reasonable persons believe that there's more to life than might be reflected in a very different epitaph that would be suitable for more people than I wish it were:

> He devoted his life to making obscene amounts of money, with few or no qualms about how, and he always made a point of spending it as ostentatiously as possible and without the slightest regard for anyone else.

On the other hand, I don't have much sympathy for those who whine incessantly about other people's success, if that success is achieved fairly, honestly, ethically. I subscribe to the view that, for the most part, we're responsible for our own destiny, for what we do with our lives.[1] I concede that fate or chance or call it what you wish does step in now and then and surprise us.

1. There is much to be said for that insightful line of golfer Gary Player: "The more I practice, the luckier I get."

A certain amount of both resilience and stoicism is essential to cope successfully with life's vicissitudes. Or as the American writer Ring Lardner once wrote: "Life is tough. Three out of three people die, so shut up and deal."

Finally, it's important for our personal fulfilment to have additional motives in life to balance the respectable but definitely insufficient ones of earning and spending money. What do I mean by this? While I hesitate to be too specific, I suggest that somewhere on the list might be things like these:

- Working to a high standard of professionalism, which means, I think, bringing discipline and integrity and, well, character to everything we do.

- Doing things for the pleasure of accomplishment, for the satisfaction from a job well done so that, near the end, we can look back with more serenity than regret.

- Putting something back into the community where we work and live, so as to help repay that community for what we take out.

In short, we might consider living our lives with a sense of service. There are many today who think that words like service, duty, loyalty, and honour are quaint, obsolete concepts: relics from some bygone age. Not at all. They are qualities that help to sustain us and to justify our swiftly passing lives.

It is difficult to be much more specific. Everyone knows that values are formed early, beginning with parental influence from the age of reason forward and proceeding through education. In detail, an ethical decision is as complicated as the almost limitless variety of situations that we must face and deal with. But in principle, it is as simple as a sense, innate or acquired or both, of what is the right thing to do.

If all of this comes across as a bit naïve and perhaps tinged with a dollop of self-satisfaction from a comfortable pew, my regrets. It's difficult to discuss this area without sounding either holier-than-thou (I'm not) or like a hopeful (hopeless?) idealist. But its importance to each of us transcends, I think, such risks.

A CASE STUDY IN CORPORATE SOCIAL RESPONSIBILITY

Ethics in action in a business setting is often referred to as corporate social responsibility (CSR). As a single and simple—at least in principle—example of CSR, I'd like to describe a case that illustrates the application of corporate ethics to a business problem that, at the time, seemed more like a crisis. It took place almost thirty years ago. In fact, it took place before corporate social responsibility and its acronym were in vogue and perhaps even before the term was coined.

The Setting

In 1942, a Canadian Crown Corporation was formed to produce synthetic rubber to replace the natural rubber lost to the Allies as Japan overran the plantations of Malaysia. It was named Polymer Corporation.

In 1971, the Canada Development Corporation (CDC) was formed by a federal Liberal government, after long and controversial debate, to operate for profit in the private sector but also to help achieve a number of public-sector goals. The first significant acquisition made by CDC was Polymer; the name was changed to Polysar Limited. I joined the board in 1974 and became non-executive chairman some four years later.

Beyond synthetic rubber, the company produced a range of chemicals and plastics. It was global in scope, professionally managed, R & D intensive, and profitable, although earnings were somewhat cyclical in an industry characterized by supply/demand price volatility. We had a strong, conscientious board of directors, mostly senior active or recently retired executives from an eclectic mix of industries.

THE ISSUE

One morning in the autumn of 1976, each of us woke up to read with horror a front-page headline in Canada's *Globe and Mail.* It trumpeted a public release from the then–Auditor General Maxwell Henderson that described certain irregularities in Polysar's European operations. When the story broke, corporate management in Sarnia, Ontario, and the board of directors were blindsided by the news.

European headquarters were in Fribourg, Switzerland, and there were several plants in France, Germany, and the Low Countries. The essence of the matter was that management in Fribourg had condoned a number of practices extending back to 1970. These included shipping product to one country and billing to an address in a different country, also diverting volume rebates either to another country or into a numbered Swiss bank account.

The rationale for these practices, demanded by industrial customers, included tax evasion, illegal currency transfers, and defrauding minority shareholders. Some fifteen million dollars of sales were involved. There was, incidentally, no evidence at all of bribes taken by Fribourg executives.

At about the same time as this contretemps began to unfold and perhaps partly intensified because of it, a lively debate was taking place in a broader context. There was, of course, no disagreement about outright fraud, but tax fiddling and currency transfers were viewed more tolerantly by some observers. At the most basic level, the issue was whether or not a country should export its morality to other countries with quite different moralities. The question became something of a *cause célèbre*, with vocal defenders and detractors. Remember that this was thirty years ago.

Some of those who supported the pragmatic philosophy of "When in Rome, do as the Romans do" also offered a gloomy prognosis for the consequences of eliminating the practice. "You'll lose half your European customers if you persist in imposing these naïve, simplistic views on countries that have been doing business a lot longer than you have." The epithets "Pollyanna–ish" and "do-gooder" were bruited about.

Nevertheless, corporate management at world headquarters in Sarnia, strongly supported by the board, stuck to their guns. Action was swift. A committee was struck to investigate and make recommendations. Its members were a retired Ontario Supreme Court justice, an experienced director of the company, and the company's newly hired CFO. Their investigation included two weeks in Europe and interviews with all of those involved in the scandal. Their report was a model of both diagnosis and prescription. Not only was the practice banned but a number of senior managers in Fribourg were terminated. And internal measures to improve coordination between headquarters in Sarnia and all foreign operations were put in place.

There were tense, meaningful meetings with the corporation's auditors. Why had they not uncovered the practice earlier and reported back to Sarnia so that action could be taken before, not after, the egg hit the fan?

The media feeding frenzy eventually abated and normalcy returned to the business. Despite dire warnings about the consequences of ending the targeted practice, no business was lost.

CONCLUSION

Ethical standards have advanced and improved in recent times to the point that, if this incident occurred today rather than in 1976, the corporate response would, almost without exception, be obvious and immediate. But in the seventies and earlier, business ethics were considerably less advanced. In this context, Polyar management and the board, acting in concert swiftly and responsibly, get full marks, if retroactively, for being well ahead of the curve.

PART SEVEN

SOME LESSONS FROM EXPERIENCE

Chapter 24

Directorship: Eleven Easy Lessons Learned the Hard Way

IN THIS CLOSING CHAPTER, I've tried to encapsulate what I like to think I've learned about what is now widely regarded as the profession of directorship, though it was anything but that in 1963 when I joined my first corporate board.

What follows are eleven simple cautions and pieces of advice to diligent directors in an increasingly hostile world. As with all advice, it's useful if it applies most of the time. Contemporary governance and directorship are too complex for easy generalizations. Nevertheless, here goes.

1. Accept no directorships where you have even the slightest doubt about either the integrity or the competence of the CEO, the board chair (separate from the CEO, of course), or even any other director. Resign if what you thought you were getting into turns out to be different and much worse than you expected or changes adversely.

2. Also, avoid joining the board of a company where, regardless of the quality and integrity of the management and board, the likelihood of failure is greater than your personal risk tolerance. The problem might be an obsolescent product or market. Or perhaps it's because of massive, looming shakeouts and difficult, even wrenching, structural changes. Mainstream airlines over the past several years and currently are a case in point.

   Some will point out that companies in these dire straits need strong directors the most. And this is often so. And if you're prepared to put up with the constant worry, the potential for personal embarrassment and reputational damage, and even the ever-present threat of litigation with its own risks to pocketbook, reputation, and peace of mind, then go ahead. But at least make a carefully considered decision. In many ways, the kind of resolute, even courageous, behaviour shown by accepting or maintaining a directorship in these circumstances is admirable. But it is also, at least potentially, a form of self-flagellation in which any benefits are dwarfed by pain.

   I confess that I have not always taken my own advice.

3. Join no audit committee unless you can satisfy yourself that you are fully and truly financially literate. Not marginally or somewhat but fully and truly. If financial literacy means that you've never read a financial statement that you can't decipher (with allowances for the baffling complexity of too many such statements), you're probably literate.

   And if you've never read a footnote to a financial statement that you can't decipher (again with allowances for the ingenuity of some of those who prepare footnotes to mislead or obfuscate), you're probably an expert. In Canada, there is, as you're aware, no such requirement (there is in the U.S.). Many but certainly not all professional accountants qualify and some others, but not many.

4. And then there's D&O insurance. This was covered in more detail in the chapter "A Cautionary Tale." But a few key points are worth repeating. Read both the large and fine print carefully, especially the fine print. Be sure that a lawyer experienced in this field goes over every word even more carefully. Eliminate the weasel words. Reduce the exceptions and qualifying clauses to a minimum. Ensure that up-front legal costs are covered. Avoid "Pacman" policies in which legal costs paid are subtracted from the coverage available. Ensure that the D&O limits are high enough to embrace all of the likely (and even some of the unlikely) risks in a dangerous, over-legalized world that is careening out of control. And be prepared for a surprisingly hefty premium!

   Don't rely too much on company indemnification. Many of the worst cases involve bankruptcy. This means that suppliers, employees, bondholders, shareholders and any other aggrieved stakeholder will be screaming for redress—and blood—without worrying much about the merits of their case … and certainly with no sympathy for you!

   If a company fails in today's legalistic world, the ground rules are that someone must be held accountable and, if humanly possible, penalized. In reality, companies often fail because creative destruction à la Joseph Schumpeter is an essential part of the free enterprise system. While success is the carrot, failure is the stick. And some level of failure is both inevitable and endemic in our hyper-competitive world economy.

However, this is irrelevant to those who have suffered losses and to their lawyers. In this area of the law, the North American environment—and the U.S. environment, in particular—is demonstrably more unfairly vengeful, vindictive, and downright nasty than other jurisdictions.

5. In the never-ending conflict between fear and greed, risk and reward, failure and success, strive mightily to find that elusive but crucial best balance. Avoid the extremes.

   There have, of course, been some incredible success stories out there where very long odds have paid off. That's why entrepreneurs matter. But the iron law of economics is not greatly dissimilar to the iron law of mathematics. Yes, people do win lotteries and beat the bank at Monte Carlo. But in the long run, decisions that work with the odds more than against them will serve a corporation better.

6. As a director, take nothing for granted. It's not a matter of trust but of risk management. Try to confirm supporting data, claims, recommendations, conclusions with one or more independent opinions whenever practical, though always with the knowledge of the CEO. And if a CEO resists, just rarely but chronically, your efforts to assess the validity of his key recommendations, you should begin to question whether you have the right CEO.

7. On balance, I now believe (though I once thought otherwise) that the present strong trend to eliminate stock options for

directors is appropriate. They bind directors and managements too closely together. Though both groups should have the same enduring objective—the long-run success of the enterprise—they have quite different responsibilities that, from time to time, put managements and boards on opposite sides of an issue.

One important role for directors is to provide that important "sober, second thought" (like the Canadian Senate, though not the more proactive U.S. one). This is less likely to take place and to be effective if managements with large option grants, motivated to push for short-term gains and over-risky decisions at the expense of the longer-run health of the enterprise, are supported in lockstep fashion by directors with smaller but still significant option grants.

Boards should, of course, be supportive when appropriate but should provide a strong countervailing force when that's appropriate, as with overly risky strategies that are in one of the wrong quadrants of the risk-reward matrix. Such strategies sometimes pay off in the shortrun but too rarely in the longrun to justify the risk. In summary, options for directors blur distinctions between two sets of roles and tend to skew further the relationship between risk and reward.

8. The ongoing relationship between a CEO and senior management on the one hand and a board chairman and directors on the other is obviously important. Broadly, there are three possible scenarios:

   - The relationship is ideal. The CEO and the chair/directors respect each other, recognize that each constituency has a key role to play, recognize further that the boundaries to each role are rarely clean and clear but are still able to resolve the inevitable ambiguities. In this scenario, there's little to add, except to say, "Be grateful if you have such a felicitous relationship." It isn't always this good.

- The relationship is badly flawed to the point that it's beyond repair. Either the CEO, the chair, or both will have to go. How this is best accomplished will vary widely. But it must be dealt with promptly. A seriously broken relationship at the top seeps through the organization and sours everything. When relationships are corroded, performance is eroded.

- The relationship lies between these extremes. This is typical and normal. It's where a strong CEO and a strong chair need to talk to each other about roles and turf frequently, candidly, sensitively, maturely, and with a common determination to make things work smoothly. This doesn't have to mean second-best compromises but rather a shared willingness to work things through to first-best solutions.

I realize that this sounds a little like something from Corporate Governance 101. And without a large dollop of goodwill and good judgment on both sides, it's all talk and no walk.

9. Collegiality matters. It matters a lot. But, unlike Vince Lombardi on winning, it isn't everything. That is, there are times when it's important for you as a director to disagree, to speak out in dissent and be counted: civilly, courteously but firmly, with conviction.

Sometimes other directors will join you in opposition to a management position or proposal. That makes it a little easier. But occasionally you will be on your own. That's when it's hardest.

Never take a tough contrarian position casually. And don't do it too often: better that you resign. But now and then, you'll be both alone and right. That's when taking a stand requires a lot of intestinal fortitude or what can be summed up in that revealing word: character. And that's when taking a stand matters.

10. In the higher-pitched, faster-moving, more demanding corporate governance of the post-Enron world, the likelihood of conflict is greater than ever. But, despite the need for a director or directors to dissent from time to time, the need for collegiality between a management and a board as well as intra-board is also important.

    Disagreement can be intense on substance but it must be honest and civil and "Golden Rule–ish" or "Do unto others–ish" in style. I have known corporate warriors who regard such talk as Pollyannaish but the best corporations, the best leaders, the best boards rarely if ever exceed the limits of civilized behaviour.

    Lost tempers, petulance, pouting, jealousies, pettiness, recriminations may satisfy the ego in each of us, but they have no place in a boardroom. And when these toxic qualities ooze into a governing body, they not only weaken the fibre of an enterprise but they diminish all who sit around the boardroom table.

11. Finally, a lot has been said over the years about the most appropriate balance in corporate governance between results or substance and process or procedure. Many CEOs and other senior executives are frustrated by and weary of what they perceive to be excessive rules and regulations. At the same time, many legislators, regulators, pundits, academics, and journalists are critical of bad corporate outcomes enabled by insufficient or inadequate process. And we should never underestimate their collective influence.

    Too much process at the expense of results leads to mediocrity and stalemate. It can easily become stifling. Too much emphasis on results at the expense of process is disorderly at best, disreputable and larcenous at worst. It can lead to shortcuts, dubious decisions, and outright fraud.

Finding the optimum balance between these extremes is part of the classic ends/means dilemma that permeates not only business but society more generally. The right mix is partly influenced by external forces: legislation, regulation, the media, and public opinion. It is also influenced by some amalgam of a board and a management in general, a chairman and a CEO in particular. This best balance is difficult to prescribe for in the abstract. But try always to avoid the extremes and never stop the quest for the best mix, as both external and internal environments continue inexorably to evolve.

This curious mix of art and science known as governance asks a lot of any director. But when it's done well, somehow it all seems worthwhile.

Appendix

Past and Current For-Profit Boards of the Author (1963–2005)

A.E. LePage Limited
American Eco Corporation
Argus Corporation
Brascan Financial Corporation** *(formerly Trilon Financial Corporation)*
Brookfield Asset Management Inc.
    (formerly Brascan Corporation)
CBOC Continental Limited *(formerly Continental Bank of Canada)*
Camreal Corporation
Canada Development Corporation
Canadian Business Media Limited*
Canlea Development Limited
Canron Limited *(formerly Canada Iron Limited)*
Capstone Investments Limited
Comac Communications Limited
Coscan Limited *(formerly Costain Limited)*
Decision Dynamics Technology Inc.*
Delta Hotels Limited
Enbridge Corporation *(formerly IPL Energy Inc.)*
e-tech direct *(Advisory Board)*
Florentine Shops Limited
The General Accident Insurance Company of Canada
The Greater Toronto Airports Authority
Harlequin Enterprises Limited
Home Capital Group Incorporated*
Home Oil Company Limited
Home Trust Company *(formerly Home Savings and Loan Corporation)*

Interhome Energy Inc.
Interlink Freight Systems Limited
(formerly CP Express and Transport Limited)*
Interprovincial Pipelines (NW) Limited
Interprovincial Pipelines Limited
London Insurance Group Company
London Life Insurance Company
Magellan Aerospace Corporation *(formerly Fleet Aerospace Corporation*)*
Malibu Engineering & Software Limited*
Metrospan Newspapers Limited
Minacs Worldwide Inc.
Monsanto Canada Growth and Innovation Council *(Advisory Board)*
Monsanto Canada Limited*
Neilson-Ferns Limited
Newsweb Limited*
Perigee Inc.*
Polysar Chemical Company*
Primaris Corporate Services Limited*
Royal LePage Commercial Advisory Board*
Royal LePage Limited
Sears Acceptance Company
Sears Canada Limited
Silcorp Limited
Swiss Re Canada Life and Health Canada Limited*
(formerly Swiss Reassurance Company of Canada)
Swiss Re Holdings Limited*
Swiss Reinsurance Company Canada*
Toronto Star Newspapers Limited
Torstar Corporation
Trizec Corporation
Union Carbide Canada Limited
Visking Limited

* Board Chairman ** Lead Director

(The author has also sat on some forty not-for-profit boards, task forces, and equivalent bodies.)

Index